D1616109

THE Secret OF THE Lord

The Hidden Truth That Defines Your Destiny

CHARLES CRISMIER

elijah books

Richmond, Virginia

All Scripture quotations are taken from the King James Version of the Bible.

The choice of the King James Version was based upon its continued prominence as the most quoted, read, remembered and published version in the historical life of the Western Church. Emphasis is indicated by bold-faced type to highlight portions of the text for particular focus throughout.

The Secret of the Lord
Copyright ©2011 Charles Crismier III
All rights reserved

Published by Elijah Books
P.O. Box 70879
Richmond, VA 23255

Cover Design by David Eaton
Interior Design by Pine Hill Graphics

Publisher's Cataloging-in-Publication Data
(Provided by Cassidy Cataloging Services, Inc.)

Crismier, Charles.

The Secret of the Lord: The Hidden Truth That Defines Your Destiny
Charles Crismier. - - 1st ed. - - Richmond, VA : Elijah Books, 2011

p.; cm.

ISBN: 978-0-9718428-6-1
Includes bibliographical references.

All rights reserved. No part of this book may be reproduced, stored in a retrieval system, or transmitted in any form or by any means – electronic, mechanical, photocopying, recording, or otherwise – without prior permission in writing from the copyright holder except as provided by USA copyright law.

Printed in the United States of America.

LEADERS SPEAK OUT

"Chuck Crismier is a prophet for the twenty-first century. His compelling new book, *The SECRET of the LORD*, diagnoses the source of America's spiritual and social sickness and prescribes the only remedy that will heal our land. This book is a 'must read' for every Christian who loves America"

Dr. Robert Jeffress
Pastor, First Baptist Church, Dallas
Former Pres. - Southern Baptist Convention

"I love Charles Crismier because he is a defender of freedom, but also is a defender of biblical Christianity and the Word of God. His new book, *The SECRET of the LORD*, exhorts Americans to come back to the truth that 'The fear of the Lord is the beginning of wisdom.'"

Dr. Elmer Towns
Co-founder and Vice President, Liberty University

"I am very intrigued by your book, *The SECRET of the LORD*. The subject of the fear of the Lord has been almost totally neglected in our day, and I believe that is a major factor in the carnality of believers in our day. Actually, every other part of our Christian life depends on this as the primary focus. No wonder God states, 'By the fear of the Lord are riches, and honor, and life' (Prov. 22:4)."

Dr. Bill Gothard
Founder - Institute in Basic Life Principles

"Charles Crismier has a deep love for God and a great burden to see this country turn to God in repentance and faith. He has rightly identified the fact that we have neglected the fear of the Lord, which is the beginning of wisdom. Read this book to capture his heart for restoring God to His rightful place and seeing America spared coming judgment."

Dr. Erwin W. Lutzer
Senior Pastor, The Moody Church

"With the winsome skill of a gifted communicator, Charles Crismier upnacks one of the weightiest truths in all the Scriptures. Read and be blessed; more importantly, read and be transformed!"

Frank Wright, Ph.D.
President & CEO - National Religious Broadcasters

"Chuck Crismier reminds us of a biblical truth amid the current darkness overtaking the earth… The Bible is the 'key' to unlocking the spiritual truths that are sometimes hidden from our human, worldly perspective. Chuck Crismier is a master locksmith, using this 'key' to remind us of a biblical truth—that will give you hope!"

Jonathan Bernis
President & CEO - Jewish Voice Ministries Intl.

CONTENTS

"Oh how great is thy goodness, which thou hast laid up for them that fear thee... thou shalt hide them in the secret of thy presence...."

(Psa. 31: 19-20)

A Preface and a Plea

NEAR THE END OF THE 20ᵀᴴ CENTURY, I BECAME strongly impressed to warn God's people of the difficult and challenging times coming upon the earth. Of particular concern were my American countrymen who profess the name of Christ in a nation proudly religious yet profoundly undiscipled.

As founder of Save America Ministries in 1992 and as host of *VIEWPOINT*, a daily, issues-oriented radio broadcast since 1995, a deep sense of concern about the spiritual condition of my brothers and sisters in Christ increasingly threatened to overwhelm me. The weight of the burden began to take its toll in my own physical health. Over a period of three to four years, as health deteriorated with the mounting stress from the developing picture of a spiritually back-slidden nation, I came face to face with the reality that, despite daily reasoning, wooing and warning by radio, I could not change the heart of those who claim the name of Christ. Only God, by His Spirit, can change a man or woman's heart. I was a mere messenger.

During the last sixteen years, I have been privileged to interview nearly 3000 Christian and national leaders, authors and broadcasters on *VIEWPOINT*. Since I often frame daily issues confronting our hearts and homes in the context of rapidly developing end-time events, I have explored with a number of guests their own viewpoint on the preparedness of professing Christians in America for Christ's Second Coming.

9

I have inquired of pastoral and para-church leaders what percentage of those professing to be Christians in our country they believe to be prepared for our Lord's return. Shockingly, the average response has been only 10 percent. The responses have ranged from 5% to 15%. How does this strike you? To me it is frightening! And what does it say of the rest of the nation…and of our spiritual impact upon the "unbelieving" world?

According to a recent Gallup Poll, 45% of Americans claim to be either born-again or evangelical Christians, yet our spiritual leaders find only 5 to 15 percent of these are living lives ready to face Christ at His return. The potential consequences are staggering. Terrifying!!

We are being set up for massive deception, giving all new meaning to Jesus' words, "Strait is the gate, and narrow is the way, which leadeth to life, and **few there be that find it**" (Matt. 7:14). Yet the prevailing message by pastor and para-church leader across the land is an ear-tickling message of the moment, pandering to self interest while bowing to the shrine of the Market. We are not, by and large, discipling God's people for eternal destiny, but instead are engaged in a temporal do-ci-do with the culture. Frighteningly, the fear of the Lord has been virtually abandoned as our foundation of Biblical faith crumbles.

It is in this context I write with a passion born of urgency. Time is running out. For several years I have labored with the growing conviction that God's people desperately need to be warned of the massive and multiplied deceptions now rapidly sweeping the earth. The time is now!

To write about deception is a daunting task, for the breadth of the problem is vast and the scope of potential permutations and combinations of deceptions is enormous. To attempt to identify and articulate all is impossible. The best that can be done is to present an orderly and principled framework for identifying various forms of deception and their delivery systems and to prepare the mind and heart of the reader to identify falsehood and embrace truth. This formidable task I sought to accomplish in the release of *SEDUCTION of the Saints* in 2009. Now, in *The SECRET of the Lord*, I am seeking to restore to spiritual memory a singular truth that will open a door of genuine hope in the midst of the imploding global horror that is rapidly enslaving the earth, disguised in the garb of a false faith promising peace and prosperity preached by an emerging counterfeit christ masquerading as the promised Prince of Peace, the Messiah.

It is said that fools rush in where angels fear to tread. That is particularly true when areas of potential deception cross over into or invade realms of doctrine. I acknowledge that I approach those discussions with considerable trepidation, yet I am trusting that you will not "throw out the baby with the bathwater" should we venture into thoughts that may step on some tender toes. The doctrines and traditions we hold sometimes have unintended or unconsidered consequences that may lead people into deception or into a false sense of security, deterring them from shoring up already weakened walls of spiritual defense. I ask for God's grace and your mercy as we continuously pick our way through some of these ministry minefields.

Read the pages that follow prayerfully. Be open to the Holy Spirit's tug on your own heart and mind. Remember, we are dealing with matters of destiny...eternal destiny. Let us prepare the way of the Lord together, rediscovering the gateway to *The SECRET of the Lord*.

Yours for a Revived Church,
and a Prepared Bride,
Charles Crismier

Titanic Secrets

"A tale of haunting deception hovering over history's most remembered disaster."

THE LIGHTS FLICKERED OUT, AND IN A THUNDEROUS roar, everything on the super-ship seemed to break loose. Beds and boilers lurched as the black hull of the *RMS Titanic* tilted perpendicularly; its three great propellers reared against the heavens. And then it was gone, and 1522 souls with it.

There had been no sense of urgency when the *Titanic* first struck an iceberg in the North Atlantic at about 11:40PM on April 14, 1912. When Edith Brown Haisman last saw her daddy, he was standing on deck, smoking a cigar and smiling at his wife and daughter. "I'll see you in New York," he said confidently, as his family was bundled into Lifeboat No. 14. "Everyone kept saying, 'She's unsinkable;'" recalled Haisman.[1] But the *unthinkable* happened to the "unsinkable." Emerging from the depths of the sea and lifeboat survivors is a tale of haunting deception and undisclosed secrets hovering over history's most remembered disaster.

"A Night to Remember"

It was "A Night to Remember" said Walter Lord in his classic 1955 best seller. But the *Titanic* was by no means the largest disaster in modern history. Unlike the *Lusitania* and the *Hindenburg*, it had virtually no political import. "Yet it remains the only disaster that people generally care about." Stephen Cox, author of *The Titanic Story*, asks, "What is there about the Titanic story that keeps us coming back to it? What is the significance of this story?" "You can have a real story without risks, but the best stories are those that ask the riskiest questions about good and bad. When we try to answer them, we recover our sense of dignity of human life.... That's why we keep coming back to the *Titanic* story—because it makes us think about the things that matter."[2]

We keep coming back to the Titanic story... because it makes us think about the things that matter.

It is little wonder, then, that historian Steven Biel in his reminiscing cultural history of the disaster, *Down With the Old Canoe*, speculates that "The three most written-about subjects of all-time" may be "Jesus, the Civil War, and the *Titanic*."[3]

"Buried 12,000 feet beneath the sea in total darkness, gone from a world it momentarily defined, the *Titanic* refuses to die." "It's a morality play...," observed *Newsweek*, "a biblical warning to those who would dare to challenge the Almighty...."[4]

"We're All on the Titanic"

It remains a night to forget for those who were on board, but a night to remember for the world. It is an irresistible tale of tragedy and truth. "Seventeen movies, eighteen documentaries and at least 130 books have attempted to reveal the moral and spiritual mysteries played out in the drama of deception played out before the world on the decks of the *Titanic*."

"It's a moment in time that encapsulates what life is all about," said Tullock, of RMS Titanic, Inc.[5] The Titanic wasn't annihilated in an instant. It took two hours and forty minutes to sink, during which people—rich and poor, young and old—had to make choices. "It is an interesting fact that newspaper reports, magazine articles and books published shortly after the *Titanic's* sinking referred to eternal truths," wrote Bob Garner, senior producer for Focus on the Family. Yet "most of these were secular publications," he noted. Garner had been a working associate of Dr. Robert Ballard, who first discovered the remains of the great ship in 1985, resting two miles down on the ocean floor in the cold, pitch-blackness of the North Atlantic.[6]

There are pivotal points in our lives when we are brought face-to-face with the things in life that matter most. At those junctures are choices that must be made, choices that inevitably determine the course of destiny. Deception and undisclosed secrets deliver us to the brink of destiny. "It's a metaphor" for life, observed James Cameron, director of the extravaganza film production in 1996. In a very real sense, "We're all on the *Titanic.*"[7]

"It's a metaphor" for life.... In a very real sense, "We're all on the "Titanic."

THE "UNSINKABLE"

The *Titanic* was large even by today's standards. This was the grandest of the grand, "representing all the power, wealth, luxury and arrogance of its age." "The *Titanic* was built at the height of the Industrial Age, a time when technology ruled as a 'god.'" She was promoted as "unsinkable," with her 16 watertight compartments. Several passengers wrote in their diaries that they overheard people claim, "even God couldn't sink this ship."[8]

The unthinkable happened to the "unsinkable." One deception led to another.

Yet the *unthinkable* happened to the "unsinkable." One deception led to another. Undisclosed secrets obscured what might otherwise have seemed obvious. Passengers boarded, brashly confident in their safety. The ill-fated Capt. Edward J. Smith was also boldly confident, cranking up the speed to set a new trans-Atlantic speed record, even as the regal vessel approached the well-known North Atlantic ice fields. Unbeknownst to unsuspecting passengers, no safety drills had been conducted.

The wireless operators ignored or made light of repeated warnings of icebergs ahead. Even the captain seemed complacent. At about 11PM, when the ship's crew spotted "iceberg ahead," frantic orders were given to turn the massive liner. There are few more dramatic or spine-tingling lines in the history of cinema than those of the *Titanic* captain in an earlier film when, upon news of "iceberg dead ahead," he cries pleadingly to his ship, "turn," "Turn," "TURN!" exclaiming, "Dearest God!" And upon news of having struck the berg, he utters softly, "Impossible!"

Yet the deception continued. Even though a three-hundred foot slice a little over a quarter-inch wide was scraped by the ice through the hull, nothing was detectible by anyone on board. But the "unsinkable" ship had been mortally wounded. Yet even that fact remained a virtual secret.

Still, nothing was detected by the passengers on board, even as the "watertight" compartments filled with water. Few had any clue what was happening. Many joked even when ordered to begin boarding lifeboats. Not until the "unsinkable" began listing and tilting did passengers realize they were in trouble. That which long seems "secret" inevitably surfaces to the surprise of the unsuspecting, leaving little time to take stock of reality.

"It was dreadful," remembered Eva Hart, a 7 year old survivor who, with her mother, was put on a lifeboat as her father was left behind. She could hear the screams echoing across the freezing waters as the huge ship rose, and suddenly slipped below, and all was darkness. "It was absolutely dreadful," she lamented.[9]

And so it will be when the conse-quences of creeping spiritual deception become manifested in our lives as we approach the end of the age. Pomp, pride, power, perks and position keep our spir-its falsely afloat while this great "unsink-able" ship of earth takes on water, ready to plunge into the abyss where time and eter-nity meet. The overwhelming majority *The overwhelming majority will be deceived. Secrets that seduced will surface too late. Their destiny will be determined.* will be deceived. Secrets that seduced will surface too late. Their destiny will be determined. Their mournful cries will be deaf-ening. The *unthinkable* will happen to the *unsinkable*. It will be dreadful. Absolutely dreadful. Yet there is a key…a missing key.

THE MISSING KEY

"It looked for all the world like an ordinary key, but this unremarkable piece of metal could have saved the *Titanic* from disaster." Such were the opening words in a heart-rending report of remorse in the *Telegraph* online paper published in the United Kingdom August 30, 2007.[10]

Catastrophically for the *Titanic* and her 1522 passengers that lost their lives, the key's owner, the Second Officer, David Blair, was removed from the crew at the last minute, and in his haste, forgot to hand it to his replacement. The key is thought to have fitted the locker that contained the crow's nest bin-oculars, vital to detecting lurking threats to the liner in pre-sonar days. Without the glasses, lookouts in the crow's nest had to rely on their own eyes, which were unable to perceive the disaster lying ahead until it was too late.

A survivor, Fred Fleet, was called by Congress to testify. When asked by the chairing U.S. Senator how much sooner the binoculars would have made the looming iceberg visible, he answered, "Enough to get out of the way."

Ninety-five years later, the key and its significance had truly come to light and was put up for auction. Alan Aldridge, auctioneer, said, "We think this key is one of the most important artifacts from the *Titanic* to come to light." "It is the key that had the potential to save the *Titanic*."

THE SIGNIFICANCE OF PERCEIVED INSIGNIFICANCE

For want of a key, the *Titanic* sank. For lack of a seemingly insignificant piece of metal, the world's greatest luxury liner and most of those who trusted in her safety met their demise. Dreadful! The *unthinkable* happened to the *unsinkable*.

For lack of a seemingly insignificant piece of metal, the world's greatest luxury liner and most of those who trusted in her safety met their demise.

And so it will be as the great ship of this world plunges at breakneck speed, setting new global and economic records, into the freezing and darkening waters of end-time deception. For most, it is not what we know but what we don't know, what remains "secret," that will define a destiny of destruction, both temporally and eternally. Yet we plunge proudly ahead, thinking we are "unsinkable." This is true for both professing believers and unbelievers. Both went down with the *Titanic* for lack of a key.

The key was not truly seen as a significant until after the disaster. Yet it was this seemingly insignificant key that would have provided the clarity of vision and depth of understanding to avoid the deceptively dangerous iceberg that lay ahead.

At this remarkable and unprecedented moment in human history, the greatest and most significant key to avoid personal and collective shipwreck is ignored or deemed relatively insignificant. The Bible, the very inspired Word of God himself, has become either disregarded or disdained. Yet it alone, insignificant as it may seem in light of mans' titanic achievements, provides the key to life, revealing the dangers lurking not only in the swirling waters around us but in the dark and turbulent waters ahead.

TITANIC'S LAST SECRETS

The world now remembers…again. It has been a century since the *Titanic* met its moment of truth. The tale of terror never ceases to grip our moral and spiritual imagination. Those memories are embellished with a thousand "What IF's." Yet another account has now surfaced, probing deeply below the surface discussions and the usually-repeated observations that haunt us to this day. Might there have been a more fundamental "secret" laying undisclosed at the door of *Titanic's* demise? Enter *Titanic's Last Secret* published in 2008.

The tale of terror never ceases to grip our moral and spiritual imagination. Those memories are embellished with a thousand "What IF's."

This "riveting book weaves new evidence from the depths with historical accounts to reveal dark, hidden truths about the deadly voyage." The "shocking conclusion: What happened aboard the *Titanic* that night was far worse than anyone ever guessed."[11]

In "a fresh, moving, and irresistible portrait of the doomed ship, combining…secret archives and forensic engineering… Brad Marsden…offers haunting new conclusions about *Titanic*: It did not have to happen this way. They did not have to die."[12] But why?

"The true story of *Titanic* has never been told," wrote Tom McCluskie. "I know things nobody else knows."[13] Indeed he did. He had worked at the great shipyard, Harland and Wolf (where *Titanic* was built), from 1965 to 1997. He ended

Secret archives and forensic engineering… offers haunting new conclusions about **Titanic**.

his career as the company archivist, and was the author of four books on Olympic-class ships. His access to shipyard records made him the world's most direct living link to the people who had built *Titanic*.

The *Titanic* had been flawed from its "foundation." The same flaw in its sister ships had become well apparent and major effort was made to retrofit them in order to structurally remedy their deadly affects. Corners had been cut in construction so as to reduce costs of construction as well as continuing costs of coal needed to fuel the required structural weight. Pursuit of profit compromised architectural and engineering principle. And the rest is a wake of horror defining a century of history.

The expansion joints on the deck and hull of the massive *Titanic* were far from adequate. The steel plating called for by the architectural plans was so reduced as to compromise engineering integrity of the vessel. And "every flaw in *Titanic's* hull had stolen minutes from the lives of 1504 people who might otherwise have been rescued by the *Carpathia*."[14]

McCluskie noted: "You don't design two sister ships, you design one. Then you use the same set of plans to build both of them. On the *Titanic* drawings, you can see lots of changes made by Thomas Andrews (the architect) after he discovered design flaws during *Olympic's* sea trials." "*Olympic* must have been right on the edge of coming apart."[15] "Yet *Titanic* was given only one day of sea trial after such troubling discoveries."

What about the British Board of Trade inquiry? "At the inquiry," said McCluskie, "it was a whitewash to reassure the world that British ships were safe."[16] "However, from private documentation within the company which I saw many times, they determined that it was very likely that the ship had broken in half (on the surface). It was never made public."[17]

Pirrie and Ismay, the owner and principal of the *Titanic* project, whose decisions had determined the destiny of so many, "must have been terrified when they'd figured that out [that the known weak joints had caused the "unsinkable" to collapse]. A public discussion of the weaknesses in their Ship of Dreams would have ruined them. They'd had no choice but to keep them secret."[18]

Collision Course With Destiny

We are on a collision course with destiny. Destruction for most lies ahead. Our vision is clouded. Our perspective is limited to our personal or collective earthbound thoughts, yet the Creator, the Lord of history, knows what lies ahead. He sees what is "secret" to us. The Bible is our binocular. It is the "key" that opens our vision, our hearts and our understanding to see beyond our naked human visual limitations. Yet we must value the key enough to get out the "binocular" that will enable us to see the dastardly deceptions ahead that lurk below life's surface like a deadly iceberg, waiting to destroy the unwary.

We are on a collision course with destiny. Destruction for most lies ahead.

Pastor and people, presidents, potentates and the poor are all on board mans' prideful ship, churning headlong into the darkness of deception. Never in human history have the forces of deception combined with the Devil's demonic host into such a formidable agent of destruction to lead you into perdition. The greatest warnings to you and me come from our Lord himself and from His disciples. The telegraphed warnings are principally to the church, to those who profess to be followers of Christ.

Most will not heed the warnings. The apostle Paul warned that they will be gripped by "strong delusion" and that they will "believe a lie" (II Thess. 2:9-12).

Most will not heed the warnings. They will wince silently in eternal remorse, "Dearest God." "Impossible!"

Some pastors, through proud and neglectful delay, will, like the Captain of the *Titanic* in a last desperate moment, cry, "Turn," "TURN," **"TURN!"** But it will be too late. They will wince silently in eternal remorse, "Dearest God." "Impossible!"

Most will simply plunge blindly ahead, deceptively convinced of the unsinkability of their ship in which they have idolatrously placed their trust. Hordes will trust the counterfeit Christ for a last great fling on the titanic of earth, spurning the hope and direction promised by Christ, the "Captain of their salvation" (Heb. 2:10), and His seemingly insignificant key. The carnage will be dreadful. Absolutely dreadful!

Don't let it happen to you! The *SECRET of the Lord* may well become your salvation.

YOUR KEY TO AVOID DECEPTION

The Scriptures, known as the Bible or God's Word, provide the "key" to avoid end-time deception. Yet for most its truths remain a virtual "secret." Our problem is not that we do not have the key but that we do not truly and seriously seek its significance so as to properly put it to use in order that we can be guided in our lives to avoid the icebergs of life and the massive deception that now threatens to destroy us.

Destiny will be determined by the value we place upon God's "key," The SECRET of the Lord.

This book is an effort to take out the "binocular" of God's Word so as to give a more distant and distinct view of the deception now surrounding us and of the profound danger that lies ahead if we do not make timely course correction. Destiny will be determined by the value we place upon God's "key," so as to discover The *SECRET of the Lord.*

Remember, the *Titanic* is a metaphor for life. In a significant sense, "We're all on the *Titanic*" together. We may just want to replace the earthly captains in whom we trust with Yeshua, the Messiah, the Christ, who alone is the true "Captain" of our salvation and who alone can guide us in this particularly desperate moment of history through the multiplied icebergs of deception that threaten shipwreck to our lives. In these choppy waters, *The SECRET of the Lord* lies ahead.

Bon Voyage!

Chapter 1

Provocative Thoughts for SECRET SEEKERS

1. In what way or ways are we "all on the *Titanic*?"

2. How is it the *Titanic* has become "a metaphor for life" for 100 years?

3. Why are we so easily deceived?

4. What secrets, if revealed timely, might have determined a different destiny for 1500 souls?

5. Are there any secrets in your life that may be affecting your destiny?

6. Does God have any "secrets" offered to you which you have rejected for ulterior motives?

CHAPTER 2

The Secret of Secrets

"He that dwelleth in the secret place shall abide under the shadow of the Almighty" (Psa. 91:1).

SECRETS ARE SEDUCTIVE! MAN'S MIND IS SUCH THAT most men and women seem to have an insatiable desire to obtain inside information on things that are perceived to be generally hidden from others. We want to be "in the know." Often our secret desire is for personal gain, but is seldom for public good. Secrets are a primary source of gossip, yet can also serve to reveal gospel truth.

SECRETS ARE SECRET. A secret is perceived to be a *secret* precisely because it is perceived to be generally unknown, unavailable or unattainable, either to me personally, to most generally or to all generically. Yet secrets are generally believed to contain information that is highly desirable, either for good or for ill. It is our natural inclination to seek revelation of that which is believed to be "secret."

SECRETS ARE LIKE MYSTERIES. A mystery cries to be mastered. It remains a mystery until the right connections of fact are discerned, unveiling truth that sweeps away the shroud of "mystery." So it is with secrets. A secret remains "secret" only so long as the truth of the matter remains hidden or unknown. Once uncovered, the secret is no longer "secret" but becomes part of the reservoir of the discoverer's decision-making ability for life direction, either for destruction or for desirable destiny.

SECRETS EITHER DIRECT OR DECEIVE. All secrets are not created equal. Many secrets are salacious, revealing unbecoming behavior. Some secrets are maintained in order to protect and secure a discovery from wrongful duplication. Some secrets are actually not secrets at all, but rather are designed as "secret" in order to mis-direct or deceive. Yet other secrets are intended to be discovered by the right persons under the right circumstances in order to provide and secure desirable life direction and even destiny.

SECRETS CAN BE SERVANTS OR MASTERS. A secret can be an unbearable burden or encompass the prospect of unspeakable joy. Many a person or family has protected a family or business secret that has hidden, yet perpetuated, untold pain and destruction. Others carry secrets awaiting with joyful expectation the opportunity to reveal the "secret" to all so that the blessing can continue to spill out upon all in the appropriate sphere. Secret sin is a dictatorial and vicious taskmaster. But *The Secret of the Lord* is a delightful revelation, bringing vitality and victory to all who discover it.

***THE SECRET OF THE LORD* IS DISCOVERABLE.** God's secret remains "secret" only to those who fail to search for it with all their hearts. Your Creator wants you to discover *The*

Secret of the Lord. But time is short. The secret must be sought earnestly and with a whole heart.

SECRETS CAN BE COSTLY. Secrets are marketing methods. Our magazines and media are filled with the promise of revealed secrets…for a price, of course. The proffered "secrets" proliferate, luring the susceptible and unsuspecting to invest their resources in the latest beauty secrets, business secrets, sex secrets and success secrets. Secrets can be costly, and most pursue them. But what of *The Secret of the Lord?* What is it worth to you? Believe it or not, your very destiny will be determined by whether or not you have discovered *The Secret of the Lord.*

Join me now in pulling the veil of secrecy away, uncovering the greatest of all secrets.

Chapter 2

PROVOCATIVE THOUGHTS FOR
SECRET SEEKERS

1. In what ways are secrets seductive?

2. What makes secrets like mysteries?

3. How can secrets be costly?

4. If *The SECRET of the Lord* is desirable, why do most people fail to discover it?

CHAPTER 3

If Only…

"Who may abide the day of his coming? and who shall stand when he appeareth" (Mal. 3:2)?

IF ONLY I HAD KNOWN…. THESE ARE SOME OF HIStory's most repeated and lamentable words. How would things have been different? Would my choices have changed? Perhaps I might have been spared calamity. Or maybe I would have experienced life-changing prosperity, blessing, or healing of body, soul and spirit. More than likely, my decisions would have been different, as would my destiny. If only….

At first the words seem pathetic, potentially dredging up a whole catalogue of missed joys and opportunities, stirring painful memories. But the words *if only* imply that if the information I missed had been either known, properly understood or properly applied, decisions and destiny would likely have been dramatically different. This is the power and potential of a secret, either for good or ill.

A SECRET

That which is *secret* is either unknown or its significance unrealized. Regardless of who else may know the truth, it remains as if it were a *secret* to the uninformed or undiscerning.

A secret is, therefore, something hidden from knowledge or view to others. It may be known only to a single person or to a select few. It remains something beyond understanding or explanation to most. It is as if it were "a mystery."

A secret is beyond ordinary understanding. It may operate in a hidden or confidential manner. It may be a method, formula or information upon which success is based. Its revelation provides answers and explanations for things otherwise unknown. Many things in life remain a virtual secret to most people! Those people who remain "in the dark" are unable to take advantage of the "secret" information which may have opened insight to change life direction; either to avoid unnecessary pain or to achieve unprecedented prosperity. That which is now seemingly "secret" may actually save…or lead to unsuspecting sorrow.

THE MOST POWERFUL SECRET

In the pages that follow, your eyes will be opened to the most powerful secret in human history. It is a secret known only to a relative few. It is a secret so powerful that it has been successfully counterfeited, leading millions to unsuspecting destruction and remorse.

Your eyes will be opened to the most powerful secret in human history…a secret known only to a relative few.

It has been said that everyone wants to know a secret. That is a truism, but is not always true. In reality, most of us want to become privy to secrets we ought not know, yet we shy away from or even reject those secrets we surely ought to know. So it is with God's Secret.

God's Secret

It may be difficult to believe or fathom that God has a secret. Some may think that it would be cruel for God to keep a secret. But what if you knew that He yearned to disclose that secret to you if you would only meet His conditions? Would you be willing to meet those conditions? Or would you scorn His secret, hoping for the best your senses and feeble scientific efforts could muster?

In fact, God does indeed have a secret. How do we know? He said so. Here is what He said.

> *The secret of the Lord is with them that fear him; and*
> *he will show them his covenant (Psalm 25:14).*

The Bible is God's Word. It is His self-revelation to His creation, to you and to me. He wants us to understand His mind and heart so that ours might be re-connected with His, both in this life and in the life to come.

God does not want you or me to know everything. He said so. There are secrets we should know and there are secrets God intends to keep to Himself.

> *The secret things belong unto the Lord our God: but*
> *those things which are revealed belong unto us and to*
> *our children for ever, that we may do all the words of*
> *this law (Deut. 29:29).*

There are things God wants us to know and things that are unnecessary, from His viewpoint, that we know. But there is one particular item God singled out, calling it "the secret of the Lord." And God also made clear the single

God made clear the single condition upon which that life-changing, destiny-determining secret would be revealed.

condition upon which that life-changing, destiny-determining secret would be revealed. The condition is clearly stated in Psalm 25:14. It is called "The Fear of the Lord."

THE FEAR OF THE LORD

The word fear is not "religiously correct" when applied to God in our generation. Yet throughout the centuries, both before and after the birth of Christ, among both Jew and Gentile, the concept of the "fear of God" was almost a given. Today the very concept is often mocked among both Jew and Gentile... even among professing Christians. Why is that? Could it be that the citizens of earth are being set up to embrace a counterfeit fear of a counterfeit christ through a counterfeit prophet?

God's final message to those of us on planet earth will be delivered by angels, setting forth His conditions for revelation of His secret.

As we sit poised on the threshold of the Second Coming of Christ, does it not seem strange that the world, and even professing Christians and their pastors, should be either passively or even aggressively rejecting the very thing that God disclosed is the key to unlock His secret?

So great is God's desire that you and I understand and embrace His secret, that His final message to those of us on planet earth will be delivered by angels, setting forth His conditions for revelation of His secret.

Are you interested in knowing and applying God's secret, or will you be one of untold millions who will embrace a counterfeit and lament throughout eternity..."If only...?"

Chapter 3

PROVOCATIVE THOUGHTS FOR
SECRET SEEKERS

1. Why are the words "IF ONLY" so painful?

2. How do we know that God has a secret?

3. In what way is "the fear of the Lord" directly connected with discovering God's "secret?"

4. Do you have any explanation for why the phrase "the fear of the Lord" has become so despised and rejected in Western culture, even among professing Christians?

CHAPTER 4

False Secrets

"But evil men and seducers shall wax worse and worse, deceiving and being deceived" (II Tim. 3:13).

COUNTERFEITING SECRETS IS SERIOUS BUSINESS! YET it happens all the time. In fact, counterfeiting secrets is not only serious business…it is BIG business. It is big business because it is lucrative…very lucrative…and successful. Consider…if God has a secret of immense value and importance, who would have an interest in counterfeiting it?

> *If God has a secret of immense value and importance, who would have an interest in counterfeiting it?*

Wherever that which is "real" exists, that which is false or a pretense of the *real* will soon become available. That is true both for products and for principles, both in matters of commerce and in matters of faith. And we are easily seduced to embrace the counterfeit. It always appears cheaper, more easily attainable. It gives the aura or feeling of having the real without paying the price.

SYNTHETIC AUTHENTICITY

It has been declared one of the ten biggest ideas that are changing our world. In its March 24, 2008, issue, *TIME* magazine shockingly, yet unblushingly, disclosed the "synthetic authenticity" that has become paramount in popular culture and in business.

The renowned authors of *Authenticity* (Harvard Business School Press) contend that to be truly "authentic" as a business or individual "puts a bulls-eye on your back" because of greater scrutiny by others requiring that behavior conform to alleged belief...that you are what you say, and say what you are. Therefore these business gurus unabashedly declare, "The best strategy for many companies is to openly fake it...." As a culture we clearly are being seduced to counterfeit that which is real and costly so as to create the perception that we possess the real.

It is truly a fascinating concept. Get real by faking it.

It is truly a fascinating concept. Get real by faking it. Yet strange as it may seem, that same methodology and spirit now governing the business and marketing world has been largely embraced even within the "Christian" world. People desperately desire...and even pursue...the feeling of spirituality while re-defining the underlying faith that produces not only a feeling but the genuine article of faith.

COUNTERFEITING GOD

The recent emergence of the terms "people of faith" or "faith-based" are merely a cultural means of purporting to "authenticate" a person's or group's feelings as the real article of faith; all feelings and beliefs are now being considered co-equal under the unholy trinity of political correctness, religious pluralism and multi-culturalism. All of this "emerging" faith and "emergent" Christianity has dramatically shifted historical beliefs about life, God and the very concepts of heaven, hell, holy living and the hope of eternal salvation versus the horror of eternal damnation.

So great has been this tectonic shift within American and Western society that God himself has been re-defined, re-imagined and even re-created, if such a thing were possible. *TIME* in its April 5, 1993, edition, diagnosed the spiritual condition as "The generation that forgot God." Shockingly, it took a liberal news magazine to measure the aftershocks of the momentous spiritual earthquake that struck America and the entire western world in the 1960's. It was a "truth-quake" of unprecedented magnitude; rating "10" on the spiritual *Richter* scale. Biblical faith was badly shaken, and the life-giving faith of millions destroyed.

The problem was not the absence of *faith*, but re-defining faith as *feelings*. The problem was not absence of belief IN God but refusal to **believe** God as disclosed in the Bible. But more precisely, the problem was not whether God created man, but that man was creating God. Churches were being flooded after Gulf War I. And *TIME* observed "Church would never again be the same." Why? Again *TIME* pierced to the heart with its poignant diagnosis…"Church will never again be the same because Americans are creating a custom-made God, one made in their own image."

A counterfeit "God" requires a counterfeit "gospel."

It was "synthetic authenticity." We want the semblance of the real but reject the substance. We want God but not the God of the Bible. We want what we want. And as consumers of *faith*, it must conform both to our fleeting feelings and to the new fake-real faith receiving the cultural stamp of *authenticity* and approval.

Counterfeit "Gospel"

A counterfeit "God" requires a counterfeit "gospel." When the Market defines or re-defines the Master, both method and message change. But is it "change we can believe in?" The word *gospel* means good news. But is it "good news" to embrace a re-defined and re-designed "gospel" that is cheaply synthesized according to our fickle feelings while rejecting the costly gospel that provides true hope in the face of prophesied horrors?

Counterfeiting has consequences. Counterfeit currency may appear (or even *feel*) real, but it is, in fact, worthless. Most people would not knowingly exchange genuine currency for a counterfeit. So then why are so many not only willing, but seemingly eager, to exchange the true gospel for a man-made, synthesized counterfeit? There are two reasons. Consider if either of these come close to home.

1. The counterfeit can seemingly be obtained more cheaply. It may actually be false, but it looks real and gives me the feeling of having the real without the cost.
2. The counterfeit bears such a close resemblance to the real that it can only be discerned by someone intimately acquainted with the authentic.

God's will is increasingly being counterfeited by a church and culture that is counterfeiting God himself. Similarly, the pathway to the promises of God is being counterfeited, giving the impression to the unwary that God's blessings can be attained cheaply, without conforming to God's Word and ways.

There is an enemy of your soul who would stop at nothing to deceive you and to destroy your ability to experience God's secret.

This is the critical connection for God's "secret." For as the Scriptures declare:

The secret of the Lord is with them that fear him; and
he will show them his covenant (Psalm 25:14).

If, indeed, the *secret* of the Lord is with those who *fear* him, there is an enemy of your soul who would stop at nothing to deceive you and to destroy your ability to experience God's *secret* and your ability to experience the fulness of His covenant plan and purposes.

Chapter 4

PROVOCATIVE THOUGHTS FOR
SECRET SEEKERS

1. Do you believe there is an enemy of your soul that is determined to steal or hide from you the secret God desires to disclose?

2. Why are we so prone to accept counterfeits?

3. Can you think of any ways you have been captured by the cultural concept of "synthetic authenticity?"

4. Are there any ways in which you may have become unwittingly participant in the massive cultural re-defining and re-creating of God in our own image?

5. What are the consequences and affects of a major earthquake? Can you relate to a "truth quake?" How?

CHAPTER 5

Your Secret Enemy

*"The froward [perverse] is abomination to the Lord:
but His secret is with the righteous" (Prov. 3:32).*

YOU HAVE A SECRET ENEMY. HE IS ACTIVELY, THOUGH surreptitiously, engaged in the War of the Ages. Your greatest enemy is God's arch enemy. His name is Satan. Originally he was called Lucifer, meaning "the son of the morning" (Isa. 14:12). He was created by God, "full of wisdom, and perfect in beauty." He was "perfect" in his ways "from the day he was created, till iniquity was found in him" (Ezek. 28:11-15). And what was that "iniquity?"

Lucifer's *iniquity* was pride and self-exaltation. Because of his beauty and exalted role in the heavenlies, he began to see himself more highly than he ought to think. In fact, he envied God, his Creator, and began entertaining competitive contemplations about his place and purpose in God's plan. The Bible reveals the iniquitous cogitations of his mind and heart

He was "perfect" in his ways "from the day he was created, till iniquity was found in him" …And what was that "iniquity?"

41

that brought him down, causing Lucifer to fall from the most exalted of God's creation to becoming the arch enemy of the Creator. These words have great import for us today…for you… if we are to find and faithfully embrace the *Secret of the Lord.*

How art thou fallen from heaven O Lucifer, son of the morning!

For thou hast said in thine heart, I will ascend into heaven, I will exalt my throne above the stars of God…

I will ascend above the heights of the clouds; I will be like the most High (Isa. 14:12-14).

Who would be feared? Who would have the awesome respect of all creation…God…or Satan?

The God-exalted Lucifer became known in Scripture as the self-exalted Satan. God, the Creator, vowed to bring Lucifer off of his spiritual "high horse," which Lucifer did not take kindly. The "war of the ages" would begin. Who would be feared? Who would have the awesome respect of all creation…God…or Satan? The battle would begin in the heavenlies but would wreak havoc on earth. Satan would be cast down and become "the prince of the power of the air" (Eph. 2:2), the "prince of this world" (John 12:31), who would bring God's wrath not only upon himself but "upon the children of disobedience" (Eph. 5:6, Col. 3:6). We must observe and heed carefully the cause of the conflict.

Thus saith the Lord God;

Because thine heart is lifted up, and thou hast said, I am a God, I sit in the seat of God…yet thou art a man, and not God, though thou set thine heart as the heart of God:

Behold…there is no secret that they can hide from thee:

By thy great wisdom…thou hast increased thy riches, and thine heart is lifted up…:

Therefore, thus said the Lord God; Because thou hast set thine heart as the heart of God; Behold, therefore I will bring strangers against thee, the terrible of the nations…and they shall defile thy brightness.

They shall bring thee down to the pit…Thou shalt die the deaths of the uncircumcised (Ezek. 28:1-10).

Lifting up one's self against God's authority, the authority of the Creator, is the cause of the eternal conflict. Satan was not satisfied to be cast out of God's presence alone for his rebellion. He took a third of the angels with him to declare a new kingdom and a new rule so as to appear equal with God. When God created mankind in His image (Gen. 1:26-28), Satan saw his opportunity, determining to defile that image by subverting Adam's allegiance to the Creator, thereby claiming the authority God had given to Adam (mankind) for himself. The remainder of human history is the unfolding story of this war of the ages for mankind's allegiance. The story will end with God's final angelic proclamation which closes this book.

> *Human history is the unfolding story of this war of the ages for mankind's allegiance.*

Chapter 5

PROVOCATIVE THOUGHTS FOR SECRET SEEKERS

1. What "iniquity" was found in Satan?

2. How does the fall of mankind connect with the fall of Lucifer?

3. How does SELF-exaltation impair access to or frustrate understanding of *The SECRET of the Lord?*

4. Can you identify the ways and means of "Your Secret Enemy?" Try to describe them in simple terms.

CHAPTER 6

Seduced by False Fear

"The Lord taketh pleasure in them that fear Him, in those that hope in His mercy" (Psa. 147:11).

WARS ARE OFTEN WON OR LOST BY DECEPTION. IF YOU and I are caught in the eternal battleground of a war between our Creator, God, and a powerful and persuasive spiritual creature, Satan, it becomes clear from Scripture that we become the ultimate spoils of that war. For if Satan has no subjects, he has no servants and no kingdom. He is our ultimate adversary, determined to link us with his deception to determine our destiny.

DECEIVED BY FALSE FEAR

Satan's principal weapon is deception. Just as military leaders seek to seduce their foes into false faith in a particular line of purported action, so Satan seeks to seduce you and me through a false faith in his word and ways rather than in God's Word and ways. This false faith is induced by false fear.

The false fear presented by Satan diverts attention from the legitimate "fear of the Lord" to a potpourri of fears that subtlety and gradually shift our trust over time. But this process of diversion begins with decision. That is how it began with Adam and Eve. Let's look.

It all began in the Garden. Life was good and simple for Adam and Eve. God had created them in His image for fellowship. Their life was environmentally perfect. Their Creator even walked and talked with them in the cool of the day. They knew neither good nor evil because they knew God and trusted Him. They were absolutely free. They needed no law nor lived under any limitations but one: "But of the tree of the knowledge of good and evil, thou shalt not eat of it: for in the day thou eatest thereof thou shalt surely die" (Gen. 2:17).

Enter, the Deceiver. Satan was determined to distract and divert this man created in God's image. His envy of their relationship with their Creator which he had lost through envious rebellion, knew no bounds.

His was a masterful deception…seemingly subtle, yet deadly. He would seduce Adam through Eve to exchange the unbounded blessings of God's eternal favor for the promise of temporal power, perks and position. They would no longer need God. They could be equal *to* God…even be *as* God (Gen. 3:1-5).

But how might this spiritual sleight-of-hand be accomplished? The seduction was actually quite simple. Satan, himself in profound rebellion against the Creator, induced the same spirit of rebellion into Adam and Eve's reasoning. Instead of simply accepting what God had said in complete trust of His divine wisdom, they chose to elevate their soulish and sensory viewpoint proffered by Satan over the spiritual authority, truth and love of their Creator. They

They exchanged a holy fear of God that preserved and protected fellowship for the horror of an unholy fear that separated them from their Creator.

exchanged a holy fear of God that preserved and protected fellowship for the horror of an unholy fear that separated them from their Creator and aligned them spiritually with the Devil, the Deceiver and the Destroyer.

They, in effect, committed treason against the rulership of God and His kingdom by embracing a fear that God's favor was not enough, that His provision could not be trusted, and that His love was insufficient to meet their needs. Like Esau, they exchanged their heavenly birthright for a mess of earthly pottage. They would now fear man. They had "changed the truth of God into a lie," and began to "worship and serve the creature more than the Creator" (Rom. 1:25).

FEAR AND FINAL DECEPTION

We, you and I, now live in the generation that will experience the culmination of history. The rebellion that began with Adam and Eve is assuming its final, fearful form in our time. The honest and holy fear of the Lord that would preserve our souls is being exchanged wholesale for the terrifying fear of man. Unfortunately, even many of our churches and spiritual leaders have become unwitting participants in the process. The apostle Paul referred to this as the great "falling away" (II Thess. 2:2-3).

The rebellion that began with Adam and Eve is assuming its final, fearful form in our time.

Consider carefully and prayerfully Paul's analysis of these times. Describing the coming rule of the Deceiver's counterfeit christ, globally warring against the genuine fear of the Lord, he writes…

Whose coming is after the working of Satan with all power and signs and lying wonders, and with all deceivableness of unrighteousness in them that perish;

because they received not the love of the truth, that they might be saved (II Thess. 2:8-10).

There are profound and eternal consequences when we choose, whether wittingly or unwittingly, to fear man rather than God. Since Satan has seduced us to put confidence in men (as gods) rather than in our Creator God, our souls become the captive spoils of the Deceiver's "war of the ages" with God. Here is how Paul defines the deception.

For this cause God shall send them strong delusion, that they should believe a lie:

That they might be damned who believe not the Truth, but had pleasure in unrighteousness (II Thess. 2:11-12).

CHOOSING SIDES

History's final moment has arrived. It is the ultimate time to choose. It is a choice that cannot be avoided. Will we fear God…or man? God tells us that "The fear of man bringeth a snare" (Prov. 29:25). Yet God also tells us that, "The fear of the Lord is the beginning of wisdom" (Psa. 111:10), that "The fear of the Lord is a fountain of life" (Prov. 14:27) and that "In the fear of the Lord is strong confidence" (Prov. 14:26).

History's final moment has arrived. It is the ultimate time to choose. Will we fear God…or man?

What, then, is "the fear of the Lord?" How can I know whether I "fear man" or "fear God?" How am I to choose? Is it really a good thing to "fear God?" Why should we *fear* God if we are supposed to *love* Him? What promises are associated with the Fear of the Lord?

These are all good and valid questions and will be answered in the remaining pages of this book. It should be of significant interest, however, that it is only since the 1960's that the very concept of *The Fear of the Lord* has become a virtual anachronism in America, even in the church. Since the birth of the nation, the phrase "a God-fearing man" was not only frequently heard but honored and desirable. Today the very concept of *The Fear of the Lord* has largely been lost to the culture. Rather than "God-fearing" being a designation of respect, it is now most often a term of derision. In our churches we are now told we should be God-loving, but the very concept of "God-fearing" is often mocked.

> *Since the 1960's, the very concept of* The Fear of the Lord *has become a virtual anachronism in America, even in the church.*

How then can we embrace "The Secret of The Lord?" You MUST choose! There is no middle ground.

Chapter 6

Provocative Thoughts for SECRET SEEKERS

1. What is Satan's principal weapon?

2. With what "false fear" did Satan seduce Adam and Eve?

3. How does Satan seduce us to place ourselves in "captivity" in the Deceiver's "war of the ages" with God?

4. Why is the "fear of man" a seductive snare?

5. In what ways does the fear of man frustrate our access to and embracing of *The SECRET of the Lord?*

The Secret of the Lord

"The Lord will fulfill the desire of them that fear Him: He will also hear their cry and save them" (Psa. 145:19).

AMERICA'S ONLY HOPE, RESTS ON RECOVERING A "secret"…God's secret. This may come as a surprise, even as a shock, to modern sensibilities. Since the 1960's followed by the inauguration of the "God is love" movement in America and in Western society in the 1970's, the thinking and understanding of both Christian and non-believer has changed dramatically. As beliefs have changed, so has behavior, and not for the better. The future of both America and the entire western world is teetering on the cusp of the forgotten truth…indeed, a "secret." This "secret" lies at the very foundation of biblical faith.

> *The future of both America and the entire western world is teetering on the cusp of the forgotten truth…indeed, a "secret."*

THE FEAR OF THE LORD

Throughout history, the concept of "the fear of the Lord" was quite well understood. It was generally understood by both believer and unbeliever alike. To be known as a "God-fearing man" was considered a good thing. Such a man's reputation preceded him, and his actions, words and ways were to be trusted. Surprisingly, the fear of the Lord actually laid the foundation, not only for a trustworthy man but also for a trustworthy society, and for the greatest nation in human history.

The fear of the Lord actually laid the foundation, not only for a trustworthy man but also for a trustworthy society, and for the greatest nation in human history.

The clear link between *the fear of the Lord* and America's dramatic surge to power and greatness was recorded for the world by a prescient secular French philosopher and societal observer. In the 1830's, a generation after both the French and American revolution, he came to America to study what it was that was causing America to leap off the pages of history into unprecedented power, prosperity and political stability. After several years of observation, he recorded his findings in his famous *Democracy in America*. His findings were both profound and prophetic. Our purpose here in reviewing the observations of Alexis de Tocqueville is not to lift up America in pride, but rather to lift up the profound and unpretentious influence of the fear of the Lord in the rise of the greatest, most prosperous and most powerful nation ever on earth.

We should, both Christian and non-Christian, believer and non-believer alike, soberly consider de Tocqueville's famous findings, recorded like memorial stones for all history.

Although de Tocqueville never used the term, *the fear of the Lord*, he did, in practical reality, describe the "on the ground" reality of a people and nation deeply gripped and governed, both politically and personally, by the fear of the Lord. He also revealed the unprecedented and unassailable blessings inuring to the American people that the world, in general, and the French, in particular, could tangibly see and even envy. But more importantly, this unbelieving Frenchman uncovered and revealed for all time the secret—the profound "secret of America's genius and power."

In *Democracy in America*, de Tocqueville noted that, after traveling the country, America's notable success and power was not rooted in her great harbors, in her vast natural resources, or in her burgeoning business enterprises. On the contrary, he noted:

> *In the United States the sovereign authority is religious,*
> *and consequently hypocrisy must be common; but there*
> *is no country in the world where the Christian religion*
> *retains a greater influence over the souls of men than*
> *in America; and there can be no greater proof of its*
> *utility and its conformity to human nature than that*
> *its influence is powerfully felt over the most enlightened*
> *and free nation of the earth.*
>
> *Christianity, therefore, reigns without obstacle, by*
> *universal consent; the consequence…that every*
> *principle of the moral world is fixed and determinate.*
>
> *Despotism may govern without faith, but liberty cannot.*

This unbelieving sociological philosopher concluded in words commonly attributed to him…

> *It was not until I went into the churches of America*
> *and heard her pulpits aflame with righteousness that I*
> *understood the secret of her genius and power.*

THE SECRET OF THE LORD

The "secret," declared de Tocqueville, was in pulpits, pastors and people "aflame with righteousness." What de Tocqueville did not know was that this was also God's secret. For the Lord, in the Scriptures, had declared of old:

The secret of the Lord is with them that fear him, and to them he will show his covenant (Psa. 25:14).

Righteousness exalteth a nation: but sin is a reproach to any people (Prov. 14:34).

In the American generation immediately following the printing of the Frenchman's poignant insights, Abraham Lincoln repeated its prophetic significance in a call to national prayer and repentance on the cusp of national destruction.

If we would...unveil **The Secret of the Lord,** *we must first viscerally come to grips with His unassailable authority.*

Lincoln declared, like a preacher: "That nation only is blessed whose God is the Lord" (Psa. 33:12). He lamented, "We have forgotten God...." He warned, "It behooves us then to come before the offended power...." But what is it that we have forgotten? That is the key that opens the door to *The Secret of the Lord.*

THE FOUNDATION OF FAITH IS AUTHORITY

The real issue in understanding the fear of the Lord is *authority.* If we would understand and unveil *The Secret of the Lord,* we must first viscerally come to grips with His unassailable authority. And the fear of the Lord is directly hinged to the holiness of His authority. Without this understanding deeply

54

driven into our hearts, we can never truly trust nor operate in the blessings that flow from the fear of the Lord. It will remain a "secret."

For the secular de Tocqueville, the connection was clear. While not spiritually discerned, the practical outflow of the principle was plain. Hence, the most oft-quoted warning commonly attributed to him continues today…

America is great because America is good; And if America ever ceases to be good, America will cease to be great.

De Tocqueville delineated America's default line. Would to God our pastors and politicians today had such discernment. For the Frenchman who had watched France disintegrate into anarchy through the French Revolution by repudiation of all authority, especially faith and family, the contrast was clear. America was built on the exaltation of faith, family and biblical authority while France had erected the Goddess of Reason. France had abdicated the fear of the Lord in the pursuit of "Enlightenment." The "secret of the Lord" had been lost. Anarchy now reigned supreme in the mind and heart of France and metasticized throughout all Europe.

AMERICA'S ONLY HOPE

America now teeters precariously on the precipice of repudiating the fear of the Lord. The *secret* of the Lord is nearly lost, and the practical problems have metasticzed throughout all American life, family, politics, and even in the centers of "faith," presenting daunting challenges for peace and security, both personally and nationally. The "secret" has been sacrificed on the altar of

America now teeters precariously on the precipice of repudiating the fear of the Lord.

SELF exaltation. Righteousness has been repudiated in favor of "my rights." The "secret" has fallen on hard times and sin reigns supreme.

Restoring the fear of the Lord is America's only hope. Lincoln called America "the last best hope of earth." But America provides no hope if We the People do not recover and rejoice in the fear of the Lord. Recovering the "secret" is the only hope for our success and salvation. It remains a matter of authority.

THE CHOICE IS OURS

Authority is the fulcrum of our faith in the God who made and preserved us a nation. We will not truly believe a God who we do not perceive as having all authority in heaven and earth. We cannot truly trust either an earthly power or God in heaven if we do not truly believe in the legitimacy of the purported authority. We will not willingly obey one we do not trust. Neither will we willingly obey one we do not perceive having the requisite authority to command or expect obedience.

Authority is the fulcrum of our faith in the God who made and preserved us a nation.

The future of America, and of any people or nation, is predicated on discovering and recovering *The Secret of the Lord.* Only to such a people, person or nation who genuinely fear the Lord God of Creation will God truly reveal and renew His covenant. The choice is ours.

Chapter 7

PROVOCATIVE THOUGHTS FOR SECRET SEEKERS

1. In what way is *fear* the "foundation of faith?"

2. How has "the fear of the Lord" served as the spiritual foundation for America?

3. Why is *authority* the "real issue in understanding the fear of the Lord?"

4. Do you agree or disagree that "Restoring the fear of the Lord is America's only hope?" Why?

5. Abraham Lincoln said, "That nation only is blessed whose God is the Lord." Do you believe that? Why…or why not?

CHAPTER 8

The Secret of a United Heart

"The fear of the Lord is the beginning of knowledge"
(Prov. 1:7).

"UNITED WE STAND, DIVIDED WE FALL" IS A COMMON cry, whether for congregations or nations. For as Christ himself declared: "Every city or house divided against itself shall not stand" (Matt. 12:25b). Yet the unity of any group or nation depends upon the unity of heart and mind of its individual members or citizens. So it is also with the church.

The church of Jesus Christ cannot be in genuine unity "in Christ" unless we who make up that Church of "called out ones" have united hearts. And certainly we cannot reasonably expect our hearts to be united collectively if, as individuals, our hearts are divided. This presents one of the fundamental challenges—perhaps the MOST fundamental challenge of our

The MOST fundamental challenge of our time is to have an undivided heart toward God that will stand against the outpouring of satanic deception sweeping the earth?

time. How can we discern, describe and disciple saints to have an undivided heart toward God that will stand against the outpouring of satanic deception sweeping the earth?

WHAT IS A "UNITED HEART?"

"Unite my heart to fear thy name," pleaded the Psalmist (Psa. 86:11). This should be the elemental heart cry of every man, woman and child who truly seeks to walk both in genuine faith and in the grace and favor of God.

The Psalmist David well understood the link between a united heart and the fear of the Lord. It is this understanding and its reverberating ramifications throughout his life that resulted in God declaring David to be "a man after my own heart" (I Sam. 16:13, Acts 13:22). David prayed:

Teach me thy way, O Lord; I will walk in thy truth: unite my heart to fear thy name (Psa. 86:11).

It appears from Psalm 86:11 that David understood a simple sequence of spiritual life that has largely escaped modern seekers.

FIRST-   I need the Lord to teach me His ways.

SECOND-   If I would walk in the *ways* of the Lord, I must walk in the *truth* of the Lord.

THIRD-   If I hope to walk in the truth of the Lord, my heart must not be divided but wholly set to obey.

FOURTH-   If I have any hope of following the ways of the Lord and His truth with an undivided heart, my heart and mind must be deeply rooted in the fear of the Lord and of His name.

So what is a united heart? How would I know or could others discern if I have a united heart? How might God make such a determination? Perhaps one of the best ways to discern a "united heart" is to contrast it with a "divided heart."

A divided heart and a divided mind go hand-in-hand. They work synergistically. James, the brother of Jesus, wrote: "A double minded man is unstable in all his ways" (Jam. 1:8). A double-minded man is a "Two-souled" man, a man or woman with a divided heart, divided loyalties, divided and insecure convictions.

Perhaps one of the best ways to discern a "united heart" is to contrast it with a "divided heart."

A double-minded or divided-hearted person is "unstable in all their ways" because he or she has no true anchor for the soul and drifts with every wind of doctrine, fleeting feelings, social pressures, philosophical or psychological reasonings, cultural changes and varying circumstances. Such a person, said James, "is like a wave of the sea driven with the wind and tossed" (Jam. 1:6). "Let not that man think that he shall receive anything of the Lord" (Jam. 1:7).

It should be obvious that a divided heart is not only unstable but can lead to decisions of disastrous consequence. A man with a divided heart and a double-mind is primed to embrace a multitude of deceptive ideas leading to moral destruction and spiritual perdition.

By contrast, the Psalmist declares: "**Blessed is the man that feareth the Lord**, that delighteth greatly in his commandments." "Surely he shall not be moved forever." "He shall not be afraid of evil tidings: his heart is fixed, trusting in the Lord. His heart is established, he shall not be afraid…" (Psa. 112:1-8).

A truly united heart, then, describes a person who is deeply rooted in the fear of the Lord, thus making possible absolute and unwavering commitment to God's

A truly united heart… describes a person… deeply rooted in the fear of the Lord… making possible… unwavering commitment to God's ways.

ways as declared in His Truth, regardless of outside pressures to conform to drifting doctrines, circumstances, cultural mandates, feelings or political correctness. The truly united heart is fixed, trusting in the God of truth. Such a "united heart" and undivided mind in Christ is blessed.

CHRIST—OUR MODEL

Prepare for a shock. Jesus Christ, the Savior of the world, had to walk "in the fear of the Lord." It is absolutely true!

Consider the prophecy of Isaiah concerning the coming Messiah.

*The spirit of the Lord shall rest upon him, the spirit of wisdom and understanding, the spirit of counsel and might, the spirit of knowledge and of **the fear of the Lord**! And shall make him of quick understanding in **the fear of the Lord** (Isa. 11:1-3).*

What was it of which Jesus would have to make "a quick understanding?" Jesus, as the God-man, having relinquished the perquisites of Godhood to become a man, needed to learn (as a man) the fear of the Lord. If he did not, he could not have been tempted toward a divided heart and mind as are we.

There is no true wisdom, nor is there a legitimate fear of the Lord, without obedience to God's commandments.

The Psalmist had spoken, "The fear of the Lord is the beginning of wisdom: a good understanding have all they that do his commandments" (Psa. 111:10).

Notice clearly the link between wisdom, the fear of the Lord, and obedience to God's commandments. There is no true wisdom, nor is there a legitimate fear of the Lord, without obedience to God's commandments.

Now we can better understand why the writer of Hebrews made this astounding statement concerning the life of Christ, a statement that few pastors will ever read or preach:

Though he were a Son, yet learned he obedience by the things which he suffered. And being made perfect, he became the author of eternal salvation unto all that obey him (Heb. 5:8-9).

Yeshua, the Messiah, the Holy One of Israel, the Anointed One, the Christ of God had to learn to walk in **the fear of the Lord** as a man, and he did so by walking in obedience when his mind and heart were tempted to do otherwise. For this reason, the apostle Paul exhorts us...

Jesus prepared for and began his ministry...in the fear of the Lord.... And Jesus says to us, "Follow me!"

Let this mind be in you which was also in Christ Jesus.

Being found in fashion as a man, he humbled himself, and became obedient unto death, even the death of the cross.

Wherefore God also hath highly exalted him, and given him a name which is above every name: That at the name of Jesus every knee should bow...that every tongue should confess that Jesus Christ is Lord (Phil. 2:5-11).

Jesus prepared for and began his ministry by developing or gaining wisdom and understanding through walking constantly in the fear of the Lord. His "fear of the Lord" was revealed in his absolute and unwavering obedience. And Jesus says to us, "Follow me!"

THE CHOICE TO FOLLOW

"They wholly followed the Lord." That was the testimony of Joshua and Caleb, the only two among six hundred thousand men whom God delivered from Egypt that were permitted entrance into the Promised Land (Josh. 14:8, 14).

They were the "sons of promise,"...but they deprived themselves of the blessing of the promise.

Think of it! God had delivered between two and three million Hebrew slaves by His mighty power from the "house of bondage" in Egypt. These were the physical descendants of Abraham, Isaac and Jacob. He had soundly set the feet of slaves on the path to His Promised Land by delivering them from the grasp of the greatest political potentate and power broker of the world. They were the "sons of promise," heirs of God's inviolable promise to Abraham and his seed, but they deprived themselves of the blessing of the promise.

They feared man, but they did not fear God.

God said they had "provoked me" (Num. 14:11). They murmured and complained continually (Num14). They feared man, but they did not fear God (Num. 13). And because they feared man but not God, they could not muster believing faith. Having no faith, they could not follow the Lord. Their ability to truly trust was paralyzed, depriving them of God's promises (Num. 14:27-30). External circumstances commanded their minds. Their hearts were divided, unstable, unbelieving. They were banned from God's blessing (Num. 14:28-29).

But Joshua and Caleb feared God, notwithstanding the external temptation to fear the intimidation of the giants in the land. God said they had "another spirit" and "hath followed me fully." Therefore, God promised to bring this believing pair into the land He had promised.

We should seriously consider the consequences of those who stubbornly refused to fear God, depriving them of God's ultimate promises. They were "heirs according to the promises" to Abraham, but they did not receive the promises due to their unbelief. God said, "They do always err in their heart, they have not known my ways. So I sware in my wrath, They shall not enter into my rest" (Heb. 3:10-11).

The apostle Paul spoke poignantly to our present age concerning the consequences of corrupted and perverted fear. He spoke of Christ being the "Rock" upon whom they could rest, but they refused, tempting Christ and murmuring in their fear of man. He said they did not please God but were overthrown in the wilderness. Their hearts were divided. Their alleged trust had been trivialized by their fixation on a false fear (I Cor. 10:1-10).

Paul then confronted us, in these end times, with an ultimate challenge...a profound warning...a call to following Christ in the genuine and uncompromising fear of the Lord that would undergird our end-time trust for the trials and temptations ahead. Listen carefully.

> *We stand continually encouraged in this end-time testing of our trust by Joshua and Caleb, who stood firm in the fear of the Lord.*

Now all these things happened unto them for examples; and they are written for our admonition, unto whom the ends of the world are come. Wherefore let him that thinketh he standeth take heed lest he fall (I Cor. 10:11-12).

We stand continually encouraged in this end-time testing of our trust by Joshua and Caleb, who stood firm in the fear of the Lord. May their testimony be carried on in our trust, inheriting the promises because we have "wholly followed the Lord" (Deut. 1:36).

OUR PASSIONATE PRAYER

The temptation to fear man is persistent. It is perpetually at war with our call to fear the Lord. It draws us like a magnet to a false master and to a false trust. It is disastrously deceptive. Yet the apostle Paul encourages us, despite his dire warning.

There hath no temptation taken you but such as is common to man: but God is faithful, who will not suffer you to be tempted above that you are able; but will with the temptation also make a way to escape, that ye may be able to bear it (I Cor. 10:13).

Our passionate and persistent prayer must therefore be...

"UNITE MY HEART TO FEAR THY NAME"

We must continually cry out as dear children to a Father we fear, but dearly love...

Teach me thy way, O Lord; I will walk in thy truth"
(Ps. 86:11).

Chapter 8

PROVOCATIVE THOUGHTS FOR
SECRET SEEKERS

1. Pollsters and pundits are united in declaring America to be profoundly divided. What lies most fundamentally at the root of the growing division?

2. The cry for "unity" has become the politically-correct mantra in both western culture and in the church. Can there truly be an honest "unity" among citizens if the citizens are not in unity of mind and heart with their Creator?

3. The Psalmist wrote: "Unite my heart to fear thy name." Do you have a "united" heart or a "divided" heart? What factors lead you to that conclusion?

4. Would you be able to recognize if you had a "divided" heart? How?

5. Did it surprise you that Jesus Christ had to walk "in the fear of the Lord?" Why?

6. What is the role of obedience to God's Word and Spirit in establishing a "united heart?"

CHAPTER 9

The Secret of Sure Blessing

"The fear of the Lord is to hate evil" (Prov. 8:13).

BLESSING FOLLOWS FEAR...THE FEAR OF THE LORD. Surprisingly, God makes no promise of blessing, success or prosperity to those who do not truly fear Him. Blessing also follows obedience, since anyone who truly fears the Lord will obey Him. This is the synergy of Scripture, resulting in genuine trust, developing love and further obedience followed by increased favor.

THE BLESSED MAN

"BLESSED IS THE MAN THAT FEARETH THE LORD, that delighteth greatly in his commandments," observed the Psalmist (Psa. 112). Wonderful wisdom and prosperous ways are promised to a truly God-fearing man or woman and family. In this chapter we will explore some of the extraordinary blessings God promises to those who, in

God makes no promise of blessing, success or prosperity to those who do not truly fear Him.

faith, fear Him. But before we seek out the covenantal blessings, we must first establish the basic conditions upon which these blessings are based.

These blessings are extraordinary indeed, but they are also exclusive. They are not relegated only to the wealthy or to those of prominence or pedigree, neither solely to the poor or to those lacking cultural stature. These blessings are neither offered to the atheist nor to the polytheist, nor even to the monotheist, but to those who fear the Lord as disclosed solely in His inspired Word, the Bible.

No man or woman will ever "earn" the blessing of God. God sponsors no entitlement programs.

To argue with the conditions is to argue with the Creator, thereby immediately becoming disqualified. Let's take a look at the simple, spiritual conditions God has placed on his blessings.

No man or woman will ever "earn" the blessing of God. God sponsors no entitlement programs. However, God in His mercy and because of His creation purpose and desire for fellowship with mankind, has divinely ordered things so as to pour out His favor upon those who crave His fellowship and cooperate with His kingdom purposes. For this reason, God is concerned with our ways as an expression of our wills. When our ways align themselves with His will, God delights in manifesting His blessings.

God's blessings are not provided on a quid pro quo basis. God is neither a cosmic Santa Claus nor a heavenly slot machine. Rather, His blessings flow through relationship. Our wills and ways reveal the true value and virtue of that relationship. While no man or woman ever achieves the ultimate sinless perfection of absolute holiness on this earth, we are nevertheless commanded to "be ye holy" (Isa. 27:7, I Pet. 1:5) and to "be ye perfect" (Matt. 5:48), because this is the standard of God's fellowship family who enjoy the blessings of His household of faith.

God is not interested in theological complexity or in creedal catechism but in a credible relationship born of truth and righteous ways. So as we look at God's conditions for blessing, we should keep it simple but not simplistic. Let's begin.

THE SECRET OF BLESSING

When it comes to God's blessings, His "secrets" are not really secret. Rather, they only seem secret because our minds, hearts and ways are not oriented toward His divine viewpoint. "For my thoughts are not your thoughts, neither are your ways my ways, saith the Lord" (Isa. 55:8). Just as children in a family do not always share the viewpoints of their parents but buck against them, even to their detriment, even so do we resist and rebel against the God who created us in His image (Gen. 1:26-3:24). We demand His love and forgiveness but resist His ways that engender His favor born of loving relationship.

SECRET #1—RECOGNIZE GOD AS GOD

The well known *Doxology* of the church universal, sung for perhaps centuries, simply states:

> *Praise God from whom all blessings flow;*
> *Praise Him all creatures here below;*
> *Praise Him above ye heavenly host;*
> *Praise Father, Son and Holy Ghost.*

This must be our life orientation. We must have a profound understanding that ALL true blessings ultimately flow from God, that we are His creation, and that we therefore should and must have a heart to praise Him. This would, on the surface, seem simple enough, but Satan (the arch deceiver) has sown seeds of sedition in our hearts, beginning with Adam and Eve. The serpent deceiver rhetorically challenged the first man and woman's relationship with their Creator with a simple question…"Hath God said…?" (Gen. 3:1). The rest is history. Satan insinuated into this first married couple's pure and trusting relationship with their Creator the seed of rebellion against God's authority as "God." The Deceiver was clever. While encouraging Eve to re-state what God had said concerning the deadly consequences of eating from "the tree of the knowledge of good and evil," he suggested that Eve elevate her own ideas and viewpoint as equal to or over-riding what God had clearly said. Satan had promised "ye shall be as gods" and "ye shall not surely die" (Gen. 3:4-5). Adam and Eve took the bait.

We are inherently prone to expect the Creator's blessing while rebelling against His authority.

Thus began mankind's historical resistance to God as "God." We are inherently prone to expect the Creator's bless-ing while rebelling against His authority. Satan put a spin on sin that resulted in separation from God (Gen. 3:7-24). Rather than walking in the perpetual joy and peace of the presence of God, joyfully submitting to His Word, ways and will, our forebearers now feared the very presence of God and hid themselves from Him (Gen. 3:8). They were banned from the blessing they had enjoyed. They exchanged God's blessing for a curse (Gen. 3:15-24).

We are increasingly confronted with the question, "Hath God said?" How we answer that question…will ultimately determine our place of favor…or of fearful wrath.

This has been mankind's perpetual pattern. It is accelerating in these hard times just before the return of the prom-ised Savior who will bring final judg-ment to the Deceiver and the unrepentant deceived. We are increasingly confronted with the question, "Hath God said?" How we answer that question in the individual issues of life that we face will ultimately determine our place of favor…or of fearful wrath. The embracing of a counterfeit "christ" and his global kingdom will be the consummate choice of history, rejecting God's ultimate gift of eternal salvation through Jesus Christ in favor of the false promises of temporal provision and blessing by the Anti-christ.

Is God really "God"? How do we recognize God as "God"? Should we expect God's blessing to flow because we believe in God? Most of the world believes in God, however they may choose to define Him. Even the devils believe in God and tremble (Jam. 2:19). But should the Devil or demons expect God's blessing because they believe in Him? The answer is clear. So then what kind of belief brings God's blessing?

God is not impressed with whether or not we believe "IN" Him. "The fool hath said in his heart, there is no God" (Psa. 14:1, 53:1). Rather, what God seeks is that we truly BELIEVE Him. This is the fount of blessing. The root of the relationship God yearns for among those created in His image is that they truly trust Him…that beginning with a holy fear they learn to love Him with a whole heart, fervently, taking Him joyfully at His every word of wisdom, for the "fear of the Lord is the beginning of wisdom" (Psa. 111:10).

Do we, do you, truly recognize God as "God"? Do we BELIEVE Him, or do we just believe IN Him?

The apostle Paul warned of our viewpoint toward God in these end times. "When they knew God, they glorified him not AS God, neither were thankful; but became vain in their imaginations, and their foolish heart was darkened. Professing themselves wise, they became fools…" (Rom. 1:21-22). Do we, do you, truly recognize God as "God"? Do we BELIEVE Him, or do we just believe IN Him? Don't answer too quickly!

When God says, "I hate divorce" (Mal. 2:16), what do you say? When Jesus says, "Whosoever shall put away his wife, and marry another, commiteth adultery against her. And if a woman shall put away her husband, and be married to another, she commiteth adultery," (Mark 10:11-12), what do you say? When Paul writes, "The wife is bound by the law as long as her husband liveth; but if her husband be dead, she is at liberty to be married to whom she will; only in the Lord," (I Cor. 7:39), what do you say?

When Jesus says, "If ye forgive not men their trespasses, neither will your heavenly Father forgive your trespasses" (Matt. 6:14-15), what do you say? When Jesus said, "Not every one that saith unto me, Lord, Lord, shall enter the kingdom of heaven; but he that doeth the will of my Father which is in heaven," (Matt. 7:21), what do you say? When Jesus declares, "I am the way, the truth and the life: no man cometh unto the Father but by me" (John 14:6), what do you say?

Agreement with God is like a symphony. Rather than our wills and ways clashing in cacophony, they sound together in peace and harmony.

Agreement with God is like a symphony. Rather than our wills and ways clashing in cacophony, they sound together in peace and harmony. Blessing follows the pattern of God-fearing ways.

Yet we are so prone to re-imagine or re-define God according to our own desires, which perverts, distorts and re-directs destiny. When we do not agree with God as He reveals himself in Scripture, we actually set ourselves up as competing or surrogate "gods." And God will brook no competition. Blessing is banned, and we are left to our own devices to create our own destiny, however destructive it may be.

This form of exaltation of man's thinking over God's disclosure of himself has profoundly invaded our churches, our pulpits, our politics and our personal lives. Within this last generation, professing "Christian" women actually held "Re-imaging God" conferences, fashioning God as a woman. The 1970's spawned the "God-is-love" movement in the church which, in exclusive emphasis of love and mercy, reinforced the "free-love" movement in the culture, abandoning the biblically-based God of truth and judgment in favor of a more "seeker-friendly" face for God. That same generation has witnessed not blessing but a curse coming upon the family which is the foundation of earthly blessing.

Even the Bible itself has been repeatedly re-translated in order to re-format God to conform to the evolving mandates of popular culture and "political correctness." When a liberal, secular news magazine finally brings focus to our idolatrous re-creating of a culturally-preferred "God," speaking like a prophet into the void of spiritual perception and God-fearing preaching in our pulpits, we must know of a certainty that we have forsaken the font of our blessing.

It was time for *TIME* to speak. On April 5, 1993, the national news magazine declared boldly on its cover..."THE GENERATION THAT FORGOT GOD." The feature article titled "The Church Search" made plain the problem. Americans were flooding back to church after Gulf War I. "But church would never again be the same." Why? What happened? *TIME* pierced to the heart of America's religious rebellion, declaring, "American's are looking for a custom-made god, one made in their own image."

If necessary, God can publish His warnings even through pagan writings when His pastors and prophets are silent. *TIME* concluded its lengthy feature article with a baneful lament.

Wouldn't it be sad that after flooding back to church, rather than the glorification of God we achieved only the gratification of man.

We must return to recognizing God as "God"...not the "god" we wish Him to be but the God that He is. It is our only hope for genuine happiness, which comes only from the God from whom all blessings flow.

We must return to recognizing God as "God"...not the "god" we wish Him to be but the God that He is.

SECRET # 2—DELIGHT IN GOD'S WORD

The real issue is authority. When we recognize God as "God," we are then in a place where we can legitimately experience **the fear of the Lord.** The true fear of the Lord, the key to God's "secret," brings us within the ambit or realm of His authority so that our ways can be blessed. His ways then become our ways, His wisdom becomes our wisdom, and His Word becomes our word.

> *The true fear of the Lord...brings us within the...realm of His authority so that our ways can be blessed.*

For this reason the Psalmist writes, "Blessed is the man that feareth the Lord, that delighteth greatly in his commandments" (Psa. 112:1). It is not enough to tacitly recognize the Scriptures cognitively as the Word of God. They must be embraced in their fulness. We must "delight" in them...all of them. Our delight must not be some abstract concept but must be revealed in absolute conviction of heart and mind. It is a daily endeavor.

The blessed man or woman's "delight is in the law of the Lord: and in His law doth he meditate day and night" (Psa. 1:2). Remember, "The secret of the Lord is with them that fear him: and he will show them his covenant" (Psa. 25:14). When God, the "I AM" (Exod. 3:14-15) reveals His covenant, and we walk in it, blessing will become our heritage. "Blessed are they that keep his testimonies, and that seek him with a whole heart" (Psa. 119:2). "Then shall I not be ashamed, when I have respect unto ALL thy commandments" (Psa. 119:6).

"What man is he that feareth the Lord? him shall he teach in the way that he shall choose" (Psa. 25:12).

SECRET #3—OBEY GOD'S WORD and WILL

"The fear of the Lord is the instruction of wisdom; and before honor is humility" (Prov. 15:33). To be blessed of God is to be honored by Him. Yet to be honored by God, we must be submitted to His lordship in humility.

When we truly walk in the genuine fear of the Lord, it brings us to a place of humility, recognizing that He truly is God. When we, from the heart, recognize that He really is *God*, His Word and will emerge as of pre-eminent import in our lives, leading us to obey…to be "doers of the Word, and not hearers only, deceiving our own selves" (Jam. 1:22). Blessing follows.

Recognizing that God is actually "God," exalts His authority in our lives. As we submit willingly and joyfully to our Father's authority in the household of faith, we become the beneficiaries of His blessings. We begin to trust Him.

As we submit willingly and joyfully to our Father's authority in the household of faith, we become the beneficiaries of His blessings.

Love begins to develop. We obey as an increasing expression of our increasing trust. Faith and love emerge as the prominent heart motivation to obedience. Favor increases. The relationship our natural mind spurned now becomes a righteous and delightsome reality.

SECRET #4—PRAISE GOD AS "GOD"

Most people would rather praise than pray. We are all prone to pray and praise rather than obey. Why is that pattern so prevalent in our spiritual practice? It is because of our perpetual struggle in truly seeing and embracing God as "God." We somehow resist obedience as defiling our desire for relationship and as a condition for His blessing. We claim God's supposed "unconditional love" and grace while spurning His unconditional requirement that we truly see, treat and relate to Him as "God" rather than as a cuddly teddy bear or as a cosmic Santa Claus.

Our praise, therefore, must be preceded by a genuine fear of the Lord in order to be genuine praise. The word *praise* and its various forms appears at least 179 times in the Psalms, most of which are ascribed to David who God described as, "a man after my own heart." If we are to praise God as a man or woman "after God's own heart," it is pre-requisite that we deeply honor and respect His genuine God-hood.

"God, and God alone, is fit to take the universe's throne," sang the gospel artist, Steve Green. "Let everything that lives reserve its truest praise for God...and God alone." The Psalmist repeatedly echoed the theme:

> *Praise ye the Lord.* **Blessed is the man that feareth the Lord,** *that delighteth greatly in his commandments (Psa. 112:1).*

> *Praise ye the Lord. Blessed are they that keep judgment and that doeth righteousness at all time (Psa. 106:1, 3).*

> *The Lord is great and greatly to be praised:* **he is to be feared** *above all gods (Psa. 96:4).*

> **The Lord reigneth; let the people tremble.** *Let them praise thy great and terrible name; for it is holy. Exalt the Lord our God, and worship at his footstool; for he is holy (Psa. 99:1-5).*

> *Teach me thy way, O Lord; I will walk in thy truth:* **unite my heart to fear thy name.** *I will praise thee, O Lord my God, with all my heart: and I will glorify thy name for evermore (Psa. 86:11-12).*

> *I will praise thee with my whole heart: I will worship... and praise thy name for thy lovingkindness and for thy truth: for thou hast magnified thy word above all thy name (Psa. 138: 1-3).*

Genuine praise, recognizing God as "God," delighting in His Word, while humbly obeying His Word and will are the underlying "secrets" to God's blessing. Notice! God has magnified or exalted His Word even above His own name (Psa. 138:3). We cannot rightly claim His name or the blessings that flow from His holy promises if we fail to embrace fully and follow the fulness of

> *Genuine praise… while humbly obeying His Word…are the underlying "secrets" to God's blessing.*

His revealed Word. To do so is an illegitimate and fraudulent effort to gain by spiritual subterfuge that which is not rightly ours, bringing a curse rather than a blessing.

The gravity of this egregious effort to claim God's blessings while spurning His authority as "God" is dramatically detailed in Paul's epistle to the Church at Rome. It stands against and reveals the heart of our perpetual pursuit of redefining, redesigning and even repudiating what God has said in His Word in order to serve the false gods of cultural mandates and majorities, religious pluralism, multiculturalism and political "correctness." Consider well the warning,

> *For the wrath of God is revealed from heaven against all ungodliness and unrighteousness of men, who hold the truth in unrighteousness.*
>
> *Because that when they knew God, **they glorified him not as God**, neither were thankful; but became vain in their imagination, and their foolish heart was darkened.*
>
> *Professing themselves to be wise, they became fools… Wherefore God gave them up to uncleanness through the lusts of their own hearts…: Who changed the truth of God into a lie, and worshiped and served the creature more than the Creator….*

*For this cause God gave them up to vile affections....
And even as they did not like to retain God [as "God"]
in their knowledge, God gave them up to a reprobate
mind to do those things that are not convenient
[righteous before God]....*

*Who knowing the judgment of God that they which
commit such things are worthy of death, not only do
the same, but have pleasure in [approve] them that do
them (Rom. 1:18-32).*

OUR HOPE IN THE STORM

Genuine blessing follows the genuine **fear of the Lord**. To place...or re-place...ourselves in the place of God's blessing, we must restore the **fear of the Lord**. The chief factor to which we can attribute the waning blessings of God in the United States of America is the wanton disregard—indeed disdain—of the fear of the Lord, from the Church House to the White House and from pulpit to pew, so that even our praise has become perverted. Since the mid 1960's, the American people and their pastors, politicians, professors and presidents have run furiously from the fear of the Lord in every sphere from church to culture. The sociological and financial statistics of this generation reveal the banning of God's blessing and the withdrawal of His holy favor.

The chief factor to which we can attribute the waning blessings of God in the United States of America is the wanton disregard—indeed disdain—of the fear of the Lord, from the Church House to the White House.

Regardless of where we look, we see the clear signs of divine abandonment of a nation that once was internationally known as walking in the fear of the Lord. Her praise is now pre-empted by her promiscuity and profligacy while her politicians struggle with bankruptcy. Her parents promise protection while abandoning their promise to God and their progeny through treachery, forsaking vows in reckless abandonment of the fear of the Lord (Mal. 2:13-17).

It is said that "hope springs eternal in the human heart." Yet the hope of America…indeed the entire western world…is rapidly turning to a hellish horror in the wake of false worship and daring abandonment of the fear of the Lord.

Our only hope, our only light for a future anyone would truly care to experience, is to restore the fear of the Lord in our lives, one person at a time, beginning with you and me. It will not begin with "the other guy."

Time is short! Jesus, the Messiah, is coming soon. Today, if you will hear His voice, harden not your heart. **Surely His salvation is nigh them that fear him**" (Psa. 85:9), "that glory may dwell in our land."

Chapter 9

Provocative Thoughts for
SECRET SEEKERS

---

1. Does it trouble you to know that God declares "the fear of the Lord" to be the foundational "secret" of His blessing? Why?

2. Do you BELIEVE God...or do you just believe IN God? What would your relatives, your spouse, your co-workers say? What does your life reflect?

3. *TIME* told us that Americans are creating a "custom-made" God...a God made "in our own image." Have you found yourself drawn unwittingly to re-design God according to your desires?

4. Could you honestly say "I delight in God's Word?"

5. Why is it so essential to recognize God as "God" for His "secret" to be revealed?

6. Are you drawn with delight to the word "obey" when it comes to God's Word...or are you somewhat repelled by it? Why?

7. Why would the Psalmist declare that the manifestation of God's glory in our lives and land is directly connected to the *fear of the Lord*?

CHAPTER 10

The Revealor of Secrets

"The fear of the Lord prolongeth days" (Prov. 10:27).

"THERE IS A GOD IN HEAVEN THAT REVEALETH SECRETS," declared the prophet Daniel to Nebuchadnezzar, the greatest ruler of the greatest earthly power of his day. The great king was deeply troubled. Despite all of his greatness and glory, despite the acclaimed wisdom of his court and the wisest of his counselors, the needed truth to satisfy the demand of his soul and the mysteries troubling his mind remained elusive... secret.

DESPERATION AND DECISION

Nebuchadnezzar was desperate. He needed real answers to real problems. His dream made him dangerously desperate, pronouncing death to all those of position and power who were reputed to be wise but who were unable to reveal the secret that troubled the king's soul. Enter a Hebrew slave, Daniel.

83

"Daniel answered in the presence of the king, and said, The secret which the king hath demanded cannot the wise men, the astrologers, the magicians, and the soothsayers, shew unto the king; But there is a God in heaven that revealeth secrets..." (Dan. 2:27-28).

The king's desperation presented a choice. Either he would resort to the traditional human wisdom of the day (which had, in reality, proven untrustworthy), or he would seek someone who could apply truth to his terror and hope in his horror...someone who could truly reveal secrets.

As with great kings and potentates, most people desire "secret" understanding in order to respond effectively to life's challenges and to uncover wisdom to solve our disturbing dilemmas. Most seek, yet never truly find. Their desperation leads to deception and to decisions predicated upon delusions, leading ultimately to destruction. "There is a way which seemeth right unto a man," observed the wise writer of Proverbs, "but the end thereof are the ways of death" (Prov. 14:12, 16:25). And so we seek, but do not find, truth to genuinely solve our troubles.

Most people desire "secret" understanding...to solve our disturbing dilemmas. Most seek, yet never truly find. ... Desperation leads to deception and to decisions predicated upon delusions, leading ultimately to destruction.

But the **fear of the Lord** leads us in the darkness to the light of God's truth. It directs our path in the ways of truth and away from the deceptive "wisdom" of the world and its systems. We must "DARE to be a Daniel; DARE to stand alone; DARE to have a purpose firm; and DARE to make it known." We must not deviate from the fear of the Lord, thus depriving ourselves of access to the "secrets" of life. God alone is the revealor of secrets.

THE REVEALOR OF SECRETS

SEEKING THE "GOD OF HEAVEN"

Daniel simply declared, "There is a God in heaven that reveals secrets." Unfortunately, most seek secrets without being attached to the root. In hot pursuit of secrets and solutions, we ignore the Savior; seeking results, we fail to cultivate relationship with "the revealor of secrets" who yearns for our fellowship. Genuine faith in "the revealor" becomes lost in a false pursuit of His secrets.

The secrets of the Lord are revealed only in the context of righteous relationship. And righteous relationship begins with the **fear of the Lord.** Three times Daniel is described as "dearly beloved" of the Lord (Dan. 9:23, 10:11, 19). God's secrets are revealed to the "dearly beloved." Those who are "dearly beloved" are those who seek the Lord with a whole heart, who revel in His presence, and who walk in the fear of the Lord.

It is no mistake that Daniel is declared in Scripture to be one of the three most righteous men who ever lived (Ezek. 14:14, 20). His passion was to seek the "God in heaven who reveals secrets." His purpose was to "seek first the kingdom of God and his righteousness" (Matt. 6:33). And his prayer was a prayer of repentance both for himself and his brethren of Israel who, having abandoned the fear of the Lord in disobedience, now suffered for lack of the "secret" blessings of the Lord in Babylon (Dan. 9).

If we are not living in the fear of the Lord…, we are "secret" seekers rather than God-seekers.

In this ultimate moment of history, revealed to Daniel in detail, we must seriously ask ourselves if we truly and honestly are seeking "the God in Heaven which reveals secrets." Are we seeking the blessing or the Blessor? Are we seeking the secrets… or the Savior from whom all blessings flow? If we are not living in the fear of the Lord, it suggests we are "secret" seekers rather than God-seekers. Which are you? Don't answer too quickly.

Chapter 10

PROVOCATIVE THOUGHTS FOR SECRET SEEKERS

1. How desperate are you to know God's "secrets?"

2. Are you more interested in knowing *The SECRET of the Lord* or in knowing the Lord of the secrets?

3. Do you believe your relationship with the Lord properly positions you with His favor such that He would be prone to reveal His "secret" to you?

4. What in your life ways, attitudes, goals and direction may be impairing your ability to receive or understand God's "secrets?"

5. Do you believe you could honestly be described as "dearly beloved" by the God of Heaven? Why...or why not?

Seeking the Secret

*"Now therefore fear the Lord, and serve Him in
sincerity and truth..." (Josh. 24:14).*

IF IT ISN'T OBVIOUS, MOST WILL NOT SEEK. MOST
people are not so much interested in actually discovering
secrets but in discerning solutions that enable them to circum-
vent the process of seeking. It is human nature to seek the easy
way, always hoping there is an alternative way to obtain that
"pearl of great price" without paying the price. While "salvation" may be offered freely, God desires that we seek Him. And
He assures us that both He and His secret will be found:

*And ye shall seek me, and find me, when ye shall search
for me with all your heart. And I will be found of you,
saith the Lord.*

*Then you shall call upon me, and ye shall go and pray
unto me, and I will hearken unto you.*

For I know the thoughts that I think toward you, saith the Lord, thoughts of peace and not of evil, to give you an expected end [a hope and a future](Jer. 29:11-14).

What does that "expected end" look like? What "hope and future" remains hidden or elusive if we fail to discover *The Secret of the Lord*? We begin to explore those answers in this chapter.

HOPING FOR THE HIDDEN

Hope is healthy. Hope-less-ness is a life of despair. "Hope deferred maketh the heart sick" (Prov. 13:12). The Scriptures tell us we can and should "Rejoice in hope" (Rom. 5:2, 12:12), that "hope maketh not ashamed" (Rom. 5:5), that we are "saved by hope" (Rom. 8:24) and that "through patience we might have hope" (Rom. 15:4). Yet the same Word of God warns that "there is no hope without God in this world" (Eph. 2:21), and there is no hope for a hypocrite (Job 27:8).

If we hope for that which seems hidden to become a revealed reality in our lives, it always begins with the fear of the Lord.

Hope, therefore, must be anchored not in feelings but in a genuine faith rooted in the biblically-revealed character of God. That hope finds its non-hypocritical foundation in the Fear of the Lord, for "the secret of the Lord is with them who fear him" and "to them he will show his covenant" (Psa. 25:14). If we hope for that which seems hidden to become a revealed reality in our lives, it always begins with the fear of the Lord. Let's then begin to explore some of the extraordinary blessings and benefits to be found and experienced as we walk in the genuine fear of the Lord.

FEAR OF THE LORD FACILITATES ACCESS TO SECRETS

God's covenant blessings remain "secret" to those who do not truly fear Him. "The secret of the Lord is with them who fear him; and he will show them [and them only] his covenant" (Psa. 25:14). Access to the immeasurable and incomparable blessings of God's covenant is our concern.

The *fear of the Lord* is the pathway to His favor. If we run from the healthy and holy fear of the Lord, we have, in reality, rejected His favor which releases the satisfying and saving graces of His covenant, both temporal and eternal. In the end, we must seek the Savior who alone embodies and bestows the blessings of the Father

> *God's covenant blessings remain "secret" to those who do not truly fear Him.*

through the mercies of God which are new every morning such that His faithfulness never fails (Lam. 3:22-24). Consider well the extraordinary ramifications connected with the fear of the Lord. Here is but a brief overview.

The Beginning of Wisdom
- "The fear of the Lord is the beginning of wisdom…" (Psa. 111:10).
- "The fear of the Lord is the beginning of wisdom; and the knowledge of the holy is understanding" (Prov. 9:10).
- "The fear of the Lord, that is wisdom…" (Job 28:28).

Protects from Evil
- "The fear of the Lord is to hate evil" (Prov. 8:13).
- "Surely salvation is nigh them that fear him" (Psa. 85:9).

Foundation of Worship
- "…in thy fear will I worship toward thy holy temple" (Psa. 5:9).

Root of Obedience
- "Ye shall walk after the Lord your God, and fear him, and keep his commandments,…" (Deut. 13:4).

- "Thou shalt keep the commandment of the Lord thy God, to walk in his ways, and to fear him" (Deut. 8:6).

Basis of Leadership
- "Thou shalt provide out of all the people able men, such as fear God...to be rulers" (Ex. 18:21).

Source of Confidence
- "In the fear of the Lord is strong confidence" (Prov. 24:26).

Fountain of Life
- "The fear of the Lord is a fountain of life" (Prov. 14:27).
- "The fear of the Lord tendeth to life" (Prov. 19:23).

Prolongs Days
- "The fear of the Lord prolongeth days: but the years of the wicked shall be shortened" (Prov. 10:27).

Source of Gladness
- "They that fear thee will be glad when they see me; because I have hoped in thy word" (Psa. 119:74).

Source of Healing
- "Unto you that fear my name shall the Son of righteousness arise with healing in his wings" (Mal. 4:2).

Condition of God's Honor
- "...he honoreth them that fear the Lord" (Psa. 15:4).
- "...them that honour me I will honour, and them that despise me shall be lightly esteemed" (I Sam. 2:30).

Promise of Provision
- "O fear the Lord, ye his saints: for there is no want [lack] to them that fear him" (Psa. 34:9).

- "They that seek the Lord shall not want [lack] any good thing" (Psa. 34:10).

Banner of Protection
- "Thou hast given a banner to them that fear thee, that it may be displayed because of the truth" (Psa. 60:4).

Hope of Salvation
- "Surely his salvation is nigh them that fear him…" (Psa. 85:9).

Condition of Mercy
- "The mercy of the Lord is from everlasting to everlasting upon them that fear him…to such as keep his covenant, and to those who remember his commandments to do them" (Psa. 103:17-18).
- "…so great is his mercy to them that fear him" (Psa. 103:11).

Heart of Compassion
- "Like as a father pitieth his children, so the Lord pitieth [has compassion for] them that fear Him" (Psa. 103:13).

Fountain of Blessing
- "He will bless them that fear the Lord, both small and great" (Psa. 115:13).

Promise of Prosperity
- "By humility and the fear of the Lord are riches, and honour, and life" (Prov. 22:4).

Wellspring of Well-Being
- "Surely I knew that it shall be well with them that fear God…But it shall not be well with the wicked, neither shall he prolong his days…because he feareth not before God" (Eccl. 8:12-13).

FINDING GOD'S FAVOR

To truly and righteously fear God is not to come continually in cringing apprehension but rather to come before Him with profound respect for His eternal majesty, his authority as Creator and his unmatched holiness. This is why we are told repeatedly to "be ye holy" and that "without holiness no man shall see the Lord" (Heb. 12:14). Primarily because you and

Favor begins with holy fear.

I, as created human beings, corrupted by the sinful Adamic nature, can never come before His presence as equals, we must present ourselves with profound humility. We are therefore admonished to "Enter into his gates [presence] with thanksgiving" and to "enter his courts with praise" (Psa. 100:4).

Man looks on the outward appearance, but God looks upon our hearts. The heart of the matter is always our heart. God's favor is found not in self-righteousness but in our willing submission to His righteous will, Word and ways. This is what set the psalmist, King David, apart from other men. He spoke continually of the fear of the Lord. He longed continually for the presence of and relationship with the one and only Creator, God of the Universe. And David found the favor that eludes most purported followers of Christ who have, in these last days, given God an earthly makeover to conform to our image.

Favor begins with holy fear. God declared of David that he was

As the apostle Paul so aptly urged, let us live "in singleness of heart, fearing God".... Do you live in such "singleness of heart?"

a man after God's own heart. Therefore God chose to set His only begotten Son, who had ultimate favor in His eyes, upon the throne of David, to rule and reign forever as King of kings and Lord of lords (Isa. 9:6-7).

What is your favor quotient in God's eyes. Do you truly fear Him? This question will gain increasing significance as we see the Day of the Lord rapidly approaching. But for now, *The Secret of the Lord* remains a virtual "secret" to most professing believers and a total secret to unbelievers. As the apostle Paul so aptly urged, let us live "in singleness of heart, fearing God" (Col. 3:22). Do you live in such "singleness of heart?"

Today Is The Day

Regardless of where you find yourself in relationship to God and to Jesus Christ, the Messiah, "Today" is the day of salvation. Today is the day to begin seeking the Lord and His secret. The "secret" is truly essential for eternal salvation as well as for temporal blessings on earth. You must seek it. You must seek the Lord himself with a whole heart, fervently.

Seek ye the Lord while he may be found, call upon him while he is near:

Let the wicked forsake his way, and the unrighteous man his thoughts: and let him return unto the Lord, and he will have mercy upon him; and to our God, for he will abundantly pardon (Isa. 55:6-7).

Seeking is our part. Salvation is God's part. When we truly seek the Lord with a whole heart, He assures us: "I will be found of you" (Jn. 29:14).

The God of Israel and Lord of all declares, "And ye shall seek me, and find me, when ye search for me with all your heart" (Jer. 29: 13). "Then," says the Lord, "shall ye call upon me...and pray unto me, and I will hearken unto you" (Jer. 29:1).

> *History's final hour rapidly approaches.... The fear of the Lord will bring peace; the fear of man will bring panic. The time to choose is NOW!*

Time is running out. History's final hour rapidly approaches. One can easily "hear" its thunderous hoofbeats. In such a time, we will either fear God, or we will fear man. The fear of the Lord will bring peace; the fear of man will bring panic. The time to choose is NOW!

As is written in scripture, "Today if ye will hear his voice, harden not your hearts, as [Israel did] in the day of temptation in the wilderness [coming out of Egypt] (Psa. 95:7-11, Heb. 3:7-8). God said, "I was grieved with that generation," because "They do always err in their heart; and they have not known my ways" (Isa. 29:24, Heb. 3:10).

The gateway to understanding the *ways* of the Lord is to first embrace a holy *fear* of the Lord. For this reason, "the fear of the Lord is the beginning of wisdom" (Psa. 111:10). It is the "secret" that opens the gateway to the pathway of salvation. It is the "password" that reveals access to the ways of the Lord which otherwise remain hidden or obscured.

THE TERRIFYING TRUTH

Salvation from sin, indeed all of God's promises, are "free" inside the confines of the fear of the Lord. We cannot fear man and have faith in God. The genuine fear of the Lord shifts the weight of our lives onto God's mercy. We are brought to painful confrontation with His absolute holiness and our desperate, sinful and wicked state. That moment of truth can be terrifying, for I am brought to the sudden recognition that "all of my righteousness is as filthy rags" and that I am woefully unprepared to stand before such a Holy God.

The genuine fear of the Lord shifts the weight of our lives onto God's mercy.

At that moment of truth, you and I stand in the valley of decision. Will we reject the painful revelation of our true condition before God, seeking to justify ourselves, thereby rejecting the fear of the Lord that calls us to repentance through God's kindness? Or, will we, in brokenness, confess our sin, restoring relationship with God through Yeshua the Christ that will take us on the joyful journey from abject fear to a walk of loving faith?

The apostle Paul, in full understanding of this predicament faced by every man and woman, made a statement shocking to modern "spirituality." Here are his words found in II Corinthians 5:11:

> **Knowing therefore the terror of the Lord, we persuade men...**

What did Paul mean? You may be thinking, *"Well, that's not the God I know. My God is a loving God."* You are absolutely correct in saying "God is love" (I Jn. 4:8). But the same Bible that tells us "God is love" also warns, "For our God is a consuming fire" (Heb. 12:29, Ex. 24:17, Ps. 50:13, Deut. 4:24, Isa. 64:15-16).

The fear of the Lord is not an option. It is the "secret" key that opens the door.... It is non-negotiable.

The *fear of the Lord* is not an option. It is the "secret" key that opens the door to eternal salvation and to all of God's earthly blessings. It is non-negotiable. If you, your family, your loved ones, your people or your nation has any future hope, God's secret...the fear of the Lord...must be recovered and embraced. We must make the choice: God, by His grace, will help us make the resulting life changes.

Time is short. Today is the day of salvation. Only two men out of 600,000 Israelites (heirs according to God's promise to Abraham whom God delivered from the bondage of Egypt) were allowed entrance into the Promised Land. The majority could not enter because they did not truly fear God. They knew *about* God but did not fear Him AS God. They could not walk in faith but rather embraced unbelief, resulting in spiritual rebellion and disobedience. It cost them everything…God's blessings and favor, their very lives and the Promised Land.

Joshua and Caleb alone had "another spirit." They feared God, which birthed victorious faith, opening the pathway to God's continuing favor and presence in the Promised Land. We therefore are clearly warned. As it is written:

Let us therefore fear, *lest, a promise being left us of entering into His rest, any of you should seem to come short of it.*

For unto us was the gospel preached, as well as unto them: but the word preached did not profit them, not being mixed with faith in them that heard it (Heb. 4:1-2).

Chapter 11

PROVOCATIVE THOUGHTS FOR
SECRET SEEKERS

1. Why does God's covenantal blessing remain "secret" to those who do not truly fear Him?

2. Have you ever considered that ALL of God's promised blessings are conditioned on "the fear of the Lord?"

3. Do you agree or disagree with the statement: "Favor with God begins with holy fear of God?" Why…or why not?

4. How does "the genuine fear of the Lord shift the weight of our lives onto God's mercy?"

5. What do you think the Apostle Paul meant when he said, "Knowing therefore the terror of the Lord, we persuade men?"

6. Are you more like Joshua and Caleb, having "another spirit," or like the rest of the children of Israel, delivered from Egypt but prevented from the Promised Land due to fear of man rather than the fear of God?

Unlocking the Secret

"...it shall be well with them that fear God, which fear before Him" (Eccl. 8:12).

SECRETS ARE HIDDEN. THEY ARE HIDDEN EITHER intentionally or by virtue of the mere fact that they are not readily discerned in the normal course of life or are "hidden" by our normal avenues and filters of thought that prevent us from "seeing" that which could be perceived if our vision were not obscured. So it is with the things of the Kingdom of God... indeed...with *The Secret of the Lord.*

MYSTERIES OF THE KINGDOM

The Bible frequently records the words of Jesus: "He that hath an ear to hear, let him hear." Why did Jesus repeat this theme both in the gospels and in His end-time warning in the final book of the Bible...The Book of Revelation? It is because He well knew that merely reading or hearing words alone, even from the Scriptures, will not be sufficient to properly understand their implication and application. The underlying truth will remain a virtual "secret" or mystery.

The reason we need the Holy Spirit's revelation is that "the natural man receiveth not the things of the Spirit of God: ... neither can he know them, because they are spiritually discerned."

The Word of God is full of such "mysteries." It is the very nature of scripture that truth is not always apparent on the surface but must be revealed. Revelation by the Holy Spirit is made available when we truly seek and when we seek truly. For the Holy Spirit is given to "guide us into all truth" (Jn. 16:13), to "teach us all things" (Jn. 14:26). The reason we need the Holy Spirit's revelation is that "the natural man receiveth not the things of the Spirit of God: for they are foolishness unto him: neither can he know them, because they are spiritually discerned" (I Cor. 2:14).

As it is written, Eye hath not seen, nor ear heard, neither have entered into the heart of man, the things which God hath prepared for them that love him.

But God hath revealed them unto us by his Spirit; for the Spirit searcheth all things, yea, the deep things of God (I Cor. 2:9-10, Isa. 69:9).

The "mysteries of the Kingdom of God" remain "secret" to most people, even to those who profess to believe God and to those who profess to be "born again" in Jesus Christ, because the "eyes of their understanding" have not been opened to the "spirit of wisdom and revelation in the knowledge of him" (Eph. 1:17-18). Human intellect alone is insufficient for true spiritual discernment.

Jesus made this problem plain to His disciples. He said to them, "Unto you it is given to know the mystery of the kingdom of God: but unto them that are without, all these things are in parables" (Mark 4:11). Note carefully! Contrary to popular opinion, Jesus did NOT speak to the people in parables to help them understand more easily the "mysteries" or "secrets" of the Kingdom of God. On the contrary, Jesus spoke in parables so that only those whose eyes and ears were truly open, and who were truly seeking and seeking truly, would perceive and understand. As it is written, "That seeing they may see, and not perceive; and hearing they may hear, and not understand..." (Mark 4:12, 34).

UNLOCKING THE SECRET

The Secret of the Lord must be "unlocked." It must be made apparent both in its *fact* and in its *fulness.*

Let's again take a closer look at what God has said through the psalmist, David, whom God described as "a man after my own heart."

The secret of the Lord is with them who fear him and to them he will show his covenant (Psa. 25:14).

We are told three important things in this simple verse: (1) God has a secret, (2) God's secret is directly linked to the fear of the Lord and (3) God's manifestation (revelation) of His covenant promises and blessings is conditional upon the fear of the Lord. Here is the fulcrum of faith.

Beginning to live in the fear of the Lord is the key to unlocking the "secret" of the Lord. There is no alternate key.

Understanding and beginning to live in *the fear of the Lord* is the key to unlocking the "secret" of the Lord. There is no alternate key. Cognitive belief is not a substitute. Bible reading is not a substitute. Neither is church attendance, nor even baptism. This may come as a surprise, since most of our religious experience is predicated on these practices.

Let's look at ourselves for a moment. In fact, perhaps we should look at the most "religious" and supposedly spiritually enlightened nation on earth as declared by the world-renowned pollster, George Gallup...the United States of America. In the United States of America, at the threshold of the seventh millennium, entering the second decade of the third millennium following Christ's birth, the following religious statistical facts describe the nation's beliefs.

- Over 300,000 "Christian" congregations meet.
- 86 percent of all Americans claim to believe in God.
- 83 percent claim to be "Christian."
- 40 percent claim to be "born again" Christians.
- 41 percent attend church weekly.
- 93 percent own at least one Bible—the average family owns four.
- "In God We Trust" is the national motto.

Now let's compare the lifestyle statistics for the United States of America that reflect the relative affect of faith on the life of the nation. Prepare to be shocked.

- The divorce rate in America persists at between 40 and 50 percent.
- The divorce rate among professing Christians has equaled or exceeded that of the nation as a whole for twenty years.
- The divorce rate in the Bible Belt states has exceeded the nation as a whole by 50 percent for the last fifteen years.
- The divorce rate among pastors is the second highest of all professions.

- 70 percent of all children in America's cities are born out of wedlock.
- 85 percent of all black children do not live in the home of their father.
- Co-habitation has risen over 1000 percent since 1960.
- Nearly half of all professing Christians have co-habited before marriage.
- 75 percent of "born again" Christians lie regularly and consciously.
- 53 million American babies have been aborted since 1973.
- 18 percent of all abortions are among "evangelicals."
- 49 percent of all black babies are aborted.
- Porn is pervasive! Among professing Christians, over 60% of men, 27% of women and 30% of pastors admit to seeking porn.

The most Bible-based, religious nation on earth is plagued by a total moral and spiritual disconnect.

What do these contrasting, incontrovertible statistics reveal? What do they say about the legitimacy of American's profession of faith? What do they communicate about our understanding of and relationship with our Creator, the God of the Universe? Answering these questions honestly will help us unlock the "secret," which may require major heart surgery.

Consider from the heart the horrifying, yet inescapable conclusions.

1. **A MORAL and SPIRITUAL DISCONNECT PREVAILS.**
The most Bible-based, religious nation on earth is plagued by a total moral and spiritual disconnect. Both secular and Christian pollsters and social observers have lamented this profoundly disturbing condition for at least twenty years. What we profess to believe is seldom reflected in how we behave.

2. SPIRITUALITY IS NO LONGER DEFINED BY GOD

Feelings have replaced faith as the arbiter of truth. The test for most Americans, indeed most "Christian" Americans, is no longer "What hath God said?" but rather, "How do you feel?" Therefore, the Bible no longer carries absolute authority in matters of life, family, marriage, finances or business.

Feelings have replaced faith as the arbiter of truth.

Advertising executives Patterson and Kim made this point clear in their book, *The Day America Told The Truth* (1990). In asking the rhetorical question, "Who is the new moral authority in America?", their succinct response from research was, "You are pardner, You are!" Thus, every man now does that which is right in his own eyes.

3. AMERICANS HAVE RE-INVENTED GOD

Americans are no longer satisfied with the God of the Bible. Some are "re-imagining" God as a woman. Others are re-translating the Bible to neuter God for a metro-culture. Most, however, are merely re-defining or "customizing" God to conform to their own whim in a world dedicated to "Have it your way."

TIME put it well in its April 5, 1993, issue, as Americans were temporarily flooding back to church in fleshly fear following Gulf War I. Speaking as a "prophet," *TIME* warned, "Americans are searching for a custom-made god, one made in their own image."

If God is no longer GOD, then who is he? ...Has he merely become one of us, to take or leave at will, without consequence?

If God is no longer GOD, then who is he? Is he merely a construct of our minds, evolving continually in image and import to conform to our fleeting fancies? Is this made-over "God" worthy of trust and awesome respect? Or has he merely become one of us, to take or leave at will, without consequence?

4. **THERE IS NO LONGER ONE WAY TO GOD**

This is astounding, yet true! Most Americans, including "Christian" Americans, no longer believe that Jesus (Yeshua) is the only way to God the Father. And if that be true, then what is the way? Is there a way? Or are we all on the way? If we are all on the way, *The Secret of the Lord* becomes irrelevant.

Consider! Recent polls reveal astounding facts regarding America's alleged faith.

- 75 percent of Americans believe that many religions can lead to heaven.
- Only 57 percent of Evangelical Christians believe that Jesus Christ is "the only way, the only truth and the only life" and that "no one can come to the Father" but through Jesus Christ.
- Shockingly, only 20 percent of the younger generation of professing Christians believe in the exclusivity of the Gospel…that Jesus Christ is the only way to salvation.

5. **THE BIBLE NO LONGER CARRIES AUTHORITY**

The following facts are heartbreaking, but true, revealing a radical re-defining of American "faith."

- Two-thirds of all professing "born again" Christians do NOT believe in absolute truth.
- Belief that the Bible is the actual Word of God has declined to 27 percent, "the lowest point ever recorded" (Gallup Poll). In 1963, 65 percent of Americans believed the Bible to be the authoritative "Word of God." So great was the conviction among Americans in the 1830's that the Scriptures were to be obeyed, that when the secular observer,

The near-universal attitude toward the Bible (even in our churches) is that it is to be "OK'd" rather than obeyed.

Alexis de Tocqueville wrote *Democracy in America* (1835), he noted that the moral principles and teachings of the Bible reigned with "universal consent" among the American people. Today, the near-universal attitude toward the Bible (even in our churches) is that it is to be "OK'd" rather than obeyed.

6. THE FEAR OF THE LORD HAS VANISHED.

The undisputed facts reveal a foundering faith. Genuine biblical faith has been progressively collapsing for two generations as the fear of the Lord has been rebelliously repudiated from pulpit to pew and from the Church house to the White House.

Nature abhors a vacuum. The vanquishing of the fear of the Lord ushered in the victory of the fear of man. Political correctness gradually replaced biblical-correctness. The pursuit of *happiness* replaced the pursuit of *holiness*, and now most Americans, whether professing Christians or crassly secular, are neither happy nor holy. Freedom's holy light has been nearly snuffed out by the encroaching darkness of unholy licentiousness.

The vanquishing of the fear of the Lord ushered in the victory of the fear of man.... Freedom's holy light has been nearly snuffed out.

If we would "unlock" *The Secret of the Lord*, we must genuinely seek it and seek to recover it in the face of its devastating loss. True liberty now and eternally lies in the balance. For now, licentiousness in the flesh has replaced true biblical liberty in the Spirit, making us slaves to the tyrannical fear of man rather than loving servants under the benevolent, loving fear of the Lord. Satan's seduction is nearly complete.

Chapter 12

PROVOCATIVE THOUGHTS FOR
SECRET SEEKERS

1. Why do the "mysteries of the Kingdom of God" remain "secret" to most people…even to professing Christians?

2. Do you believe that statistics over the past 30 years reveal a progressive abandonment of the fear of the Lord in America? How about in the American church?

3. Is there a moral and spiritual disconnect in your life?

4. Have you somehow, perhaps unwittingly, been part of the trend to re-invent, re-define, and customize God? How?

5. Is the Bible your absolute authority for life? Are you absolutely sure? Or have you adopted, as have most Christians, the standards and practices of the culture rather than those of Christ?

6. How can we "unlock" *The SECRET of the Lord?*

CHAPTER 13

Trust Is the Key

"Gather the people together, men and women, and children, and the stranger that is within thy gates, that they may hear, and that they may learn, and fear the Lord your God…" (Deut. 31:12).

EVERY LOCK REQUIRES A KEY OF SOME KIND IN ORDER to gain access to the contents secured by the lock. *The Secret of the Lord* remains "locked" from access without the "key" that opens the way. The key that opens the pathway to that which remains hidden may be a physical key, a numerical combination or even a password.

The *fear of the Lord* is similar to a lock. It is the "lock" that prevents or provides access to *The Secret of the Lord*. The key or password that opens the lock of the fear of the Lord is **TRUST**. *The Secret of the Lord* lies on the other side of trust. I will never truly trust the Lord if I do not first truly "fear" Him. Neither will I truly fear the Lord in faith if I do not *trust* Him.

> *The fear of the Lord is…the "lock" that prevents or provides access to The Secret of the Lord.*

TRUST IS TROUBLING

Trust is the key. There is no alternate key, though we often wish there were, because trust is troubling. Trust is troubling to most because it requires submission to God's Word, will and ways that does violence to our own sense of self-determination. It requires, in a sense, that we release our will to the divine will of God which causes considerable discomfort to our "natural man," carnal nature and soulish sense of self. Most resist the fulness of such simple trust, seeking to straddle the fence between alleged faith in God and trust in man, never fully able to access *The Secret of the Lord*.

Trust is troubling to most because it requires submission to God's Word, will and ways...which causes considerable discomfort to our "natural man."

Surprisingly, the fear of the Lord is directly linked to trust. If I do not first learn to fear the Lord, I will not be able to truly trust Him. That is why God tells us that "The fear of the Lord is the beginning of wisdom" (Ps. 111:10). Yet if I do not truly trust the Lord and His Word, I will never be able to truly serve and obey Him, thus preventing me from experiencing the outpouring of His covenantal blessings, both now and even for eternity.

Perhaps we can now better appreciate the gospel simplicity of the mostly-forgotten gospel song, *TRUST and OBEY*.

When we walk with the Lord,
In the light of His word,
What a glory He sheds on our way.
When we do His good will,
He abides with us still,
And with all who will *trust and obey*.

Trust and Obey,
For there's no other way
To be happy in Jesus,
But to *Trust and Obey.*

The Pathway To Trust

Trust is not a tangible product. It is troublingly elusive. Trust is theoretically and theologically desired by most, yet seldom attained in truth by any.

Frustrated By Fear

Genuine trust is continually frustrated by fear. Fear is the enemy of faith, forever forbidding access to the trusting relationship of rest in God for which we so much yearn. Our innermost beings, our very souls, crave to be able to truly trust our Creator, but something within continually wages war against that which our soul craves, seducing us to fear rather than to a trusting faith.

The fear that seduces us also deceives us into embracing a counterfeit "key" that persistently prohibits access to God's promises. Rather than leading to increased trusting faith, it inevitably consigns us to broken expectations, cynicism and increasing frustration that decimates whatever residue of faith may remain. Although we may be loathe to admit it, a sense of growing HOPElessness hovers over our alleged pursuit of fellowship with God, placing the true object of our desire seemingly continually out of reach. But it need not be that way. How can we escape this seductive submission to fear? The pathway lies in answering two critical questions:

Our innermost beings…crave to be able to truly trust our Creator, but something within continually wages war against that which our soul craves, seducing us to fear rather than to a trusting faith.

111

1. Why am I so easily seduced by fear that keeps me from truly trusting God?
2. Is there another kind of *fear* that is righteous, and that rather than frustrating trust actually facilitates genuine trust in God?

WHY AM I EASILY SEDUCED BY FEAR?

We are spiritual beings. God created mankind in His own image (Gen. 1:26-27). And "God is a Spirit." "They that worship him must worship him in spirit and in truth" (Jn. 4:24).

This makes apparent two of the most devastating deceptions of our time that affect your destiny. First is the belief that somehow we are spiritual beings, yet not made (created) by God but have merely inexorably evolved from primordial slime, thus eliminating God as Creator having authority over His creation. Second is the so-called "post-modern" concept that no absolute truth exists absolutely, thus rendering it possible (in our thinking) that we can be "spiritual" without being bound by some "truth" outside of ourselves.

The result of these two deceptions is that we, in effect, declare ourselves "God," being spirit beings outside of His creation dominion and being the final arbiters of "truth." There is then no room left for godly trust. All "trust" is shifted to man. And man will always fear that which he or she does not absolutely trust. Do you absolutely trust mankind...or man's best efforts to govern himself without God?

That leads us back to the Garden of Eden. The picture seems perfect. God has created Adam in His own perfect image, bestowing upon Adam perfect blessing and presenting him with a perfect, unblemished wife as his joyful helpmate. They, together, have only one restriction in their governance and gift of the Garden—they must not eat of "the tree of the knowledge of good and evil," for they would surely die (Gen. 2:16-17). How much better can life be?

We should ask ourselves, "Why did God not want Adam and Eve to eat of the tree of the knowledge of good and evil?" The answer is actually quite simple. God wanted an open relationship with Adam and Eve, who were created in God's own image (unlike the animals). God wanted Adam and Eve (progenitors of you and me) to truly trust Him. He wanted them to trust Him so perfectly, to be at such rest in their relationship, that they had no need to discern or even try to distinguish between good and evil. All they had to do was to simply take God, their Father, at His word. What a life! What joy! What peace! What fulfillment!

Then came the "serpent," the Deceiver, Satan. He was profoundly envious of man's enviable, perfect state. For Satan himself had once been the greatest of all created beings, "the anointed cherub that covereth." He had enjoyed a perfect relationship with His Creator "till iniquity was found in thee." And he was "in Eden the Garden of God" (Ezek. 28:1-19).

What was the "iniquity" found in Lucifer (Satan)? He set his heart "as the heart of God" saying, "I am a God, I sit in the seat of God…" (Ezek. 28:2). And for that treasonous, prideful rebellion, purporting to make himself equal with God His Creator, he was cast out. He took one-third of the created heavenly angels with him in the rebellion, and he is determined to take as many men and women on earth to perdition with him as he can in that continuing rebellion. But how does the Deceiver do it? It is very simple.

Satan seduces you and me to disagree with what God the Father has said, either in whole or in part, thus effectively daring us to declare ourselves equal with God. Having eaten of "the tree of the knowledge of good and evil," we now believe our thinking, our choices, our values, our goals, our priorities, our re-defining of

> *Satan seduces you and me to disagree with what God the Father has said…daring us to declare ourselves equal with God.*

what is *good* and what is *evil* either equals or exceeds what God as Creator has said.

Trust in God is broken. Our trust shifts to ourselves, to government, to our culture or to society's ever fickle and fleeting re-definition of faith and even family. Greed supplants gratitude, rebellion replaces rest and righteousness, violence and victim-hood take dominion as the very foundation of true faith is eroded in the headlong pursuit of happiness and SELFish ambition. Good is declared "evil" and evil is promoted as "good." *The Secret of the Lord* becomes hopelessly obscured in the resulting fog of fear.

RECOVERING GODLY FEAR

Here lies our dilemma. Whom or what should we truly and legitimately fear? We have a choice. If indeed "The Secret of the Lord is with them that fear him," and if to them only that truly fear Him, He "will show [reveal and manifest] his covenant" (Psa. 25:14), we have a serious choice to make. It is a choice bearing either glorious or grave consequences, both now and for eternity.

We have a serious choice to make. It is a choice bearing either glorious or grave consequences, both now and for eternity.

From God's viewpoint as disclosed in His Word, the Bible, there is no area of neutrality on this issue. It is a matter fundamental to not only the Christian faith but also to the true Hebrew Scriptures (Old Covenant) attested to by Jewish believers in the God of Abraham, Isaac and Jacob. The *fear of the Lord* might well be seen in many respects as "the fulcrum of faith."

If that be true in any significant measure, the fact that so-called "Christian Europe" and her daughter, "Christian America," each having globally-acknowledged Judeo-Christian roots and foundation, have virtually abandoned all pretense of the fear of the Lord in life, practice and politics, as has Israel, this issue is not only one of individual or national concern but portends global consequences. It should be of ultimate concern, then, that we discern how to reclaim Godly fear. Time is of the essence.

In reality, reclaiming, re-discovering or re-capturing Godly fear [The Fear of the Lord] is not difficult to understand. Little children understand it better than we adults do. The older we get, the more prone we become to abandon the true fear of the Lord. As a result, we progressively find ourselves fearing almost

The older we get, the more prone we become to abandon the true fear of the Lord. ...We progressively find ourselves fearing almost everything but God.

everything but God. For we tacitly say to ourselves, *Why should I fear God? Doesn't He want me to love Him?* And *The Secret of the Lord* becomes a casualty.

Child-Like Faith

Consider a normal family in America (before Dr. Benjamin Spock, whose child-rearing doctrine dramatically changed attitudes toward child rearing beginning in the 1950's and taking root in the 1960's). Infants were born and tenderly nurtured for several months at their mother's breast. Dad provided what care he could. The newborn understood neither love nor fear, relatively oblivious to his/her environment but concerned only for immediate needs.

As months drew on, the infant began to assimilate language and communication ability, primarily with exposure to parental conversation. At some point, most likely between six months and a year after birth, mother and father began to direct modest and gentle commands or directive comments…"come," "look," "smile." Few, if any, such directives were of any moral or safety significance. Neither did the child find within a willful motivation to resist, nor a loving motivation to respond, to mom or dad's encouragements. It was a world of moral and relational neutrality.

Then, much to parental bewilderment, both bits of heaven and hell began to break loose. The infant, becoming a young child, began to respond in increasingly obvious relationship, warming mom and dad's heart. But then the infamous word "NO!" seemingly appeared from nowhere, and the battle lines began to be drawn. Will parent and child be in loving relationship or be in a perpetual or recurring state of war? How should a loving mother and father respond if they yearn for this formerly "innocent and sweet" being to bless the family with love from the heart?

Dr. Benjamin Spock turned historical understandings of child rearing upside down. Believing we, in the mid-twentieth century, were in an advanced state of "enlightenment," Dr. Spock urged parents to be non-directional toward their children. Just let them develop on their own. Let them have and find their own way. Provide them with no real discipline, only "love."

It was known as "laissez-faire" child rearing. Parents were to take their hands off and let life happen. And indeed life happened. America and the entire western world never experienced such massive rebellion among its youth as took place in the 1960's. All of the verities of life, love and faith were summarily dismissed as no longer relevant. Having been freed from parental restraint, the upcoming generation of Baby-Busters declared themselves free also from God's restraint, leaving their children as virtual orphans, politely labeled "Generation X."

Forty years later, Burger King captured the ethos of two generations of "Spock babies" in its global advertising mantras…"HAVE IT YOUR WAY"…"GOTTA GIVE THE PEOPLE WHAT THEY WANT." The children (now adults) may think they have what they *want*, but they never received what they needed. Therefore licentious living replaced the heart yearning for love. As one popular song so aptly observed in the 1960's, "Money can't buy you love." Two generations of parental experimentation nearly destroyed our children's ability to have faith. A child needs love, but what does love look like from God's viewpoint?

RECOVERING REAL LOVE

If we and our children have any hope of recovering the real love of God, we must first recover the very concept of "love" from God's viewpoint. To truly recover that understanding will bring us into direct conflict with western culture and indeed with much of what has been promoted as "Christian" faith in our churches.

Indeed, the picture describing the last two generations of American and western life and child rearing is a profound parable that reveals much of what has happened in our relationship with God… both its causes and consequences. We have not only forgotten but refused to parent as God parents. We have superimposed upon our Creator, who is both God and Father, the perverted "enlightened" concepts of parenting promoted by Dr. Spock and his psychological disciples.

Indeed, the picture describing the last two generations of American and western life and child rearing is a profound parable that reveals much of what has happened in our relationship with God…both its causes and consequences.

The result has been devastating, not only to our earthly relationships with one another, including our politics and policies and fathering itself, but also to our relationship with God. As *TIME* so poignantly pointed out in its April 5, 1993, edition, this deceptive distortion has culminated in the necessity of re-defining, re-imagining, indeed re-creating God. Americans are "searching for a custom-made God," observed the national news magazine, "one [a God] made in their own image."

The "God" we seek is a god we can love but not fear. We yearn for a god who will give us everything we want. We pursue

The "God" we seek is a god we can love but not fear...who will give us everything we want...who will require nothing more than to "have it our way"... We demand a god who dotes but who makes no demands.

a god who will require nothing more than to "have it our way," just like Burger King. We demand a god who dotes but who makes no demands. We categorically reject any god who would dare to discipline or judge, demanding our custom-made god to accede continually, without remonstrance, to our deified individualistic and democratic will and whim.

In reality, just as Dr. Spock and his disciples made children their own parents, disenfranchising mothers and fathers of their God-given responsibilities, so we disenfranchise God from being "God," elevating ourselves as co-equal with or even superior to our Creator. We have, in effect, become "God" in our own eyes. Even our worship in our churches has dramatically shifted from a profound sense of God's holiness, in humility of spirit, to either pure ritual, so that we can *feel* spiritual, or to a raucous celebration of worship itself rather than of God as the true and awesome Creator of all, worthy of all praise.

Regardless of mankind's collective uprising against Him, God will be "God." And "the hour has come, and now is, when true worshipers shall worship the Father in spirit and in truth: for the Father seeketh such to worship him" (Jn. 4:23-24).

When we truly learn how to love God, from His viewpoint, we will have re-discovered **The Secret of the Lord.**

If we would recover and experience the true love of God, we must first relearn how to truly love Him. When we truly learn how to love God, from His viewpoint, we will have re-discovered *The Secret of the Lord.* Are you interested? Are you sufficiently interested to allow God to be "God"? Trust is the key.

Chapter 13

Provocative Thoughts for
SECRET SEEKERS

1. In what way is the *fear of the Lord* similar to a lock? To what does it provide access?

2. If TRUST is the key to unlock access to *The SECRET of the Lord*, why is trust so troubling?

3. How does fear keep us from truly trusting God?

4. Why are we so easily seduced by fear?

5. What must happen in your life to recover and maintain genuine godly fear?

CHAPTER 14

How God Becomes "God"

"Let all the earth fear the Lord: let all the inhabitants of the world stand in awe of Him" (Psa. 33:8).

GOD IS "GOD." MOST PEOPLE, ESPECIALLY PROFESSING Christians, have historically embraced that statement as a non-negotiable fact. Such is no longer the case, however, except perhaps as some vague spiritual theory.

As we have seen, God has become whatever we want Him to be, whatever our fickle "faith" (defined mostly as feelings) desire Him to be. In this "ME" generation, having parented ourselves in "child-centered" families for two generations, the great "I AM" has become little more than a cosmic Santa Claus, at the instant beck and call of spoiled spiritual children who have little comprehension of God as "God."

LETTING GOD BE "GOD"

All of the foundations of the earth seem to be out of course (Psa. 82:5). And "If the foundations be destroyed, what can the righteous do" (Psa. 11:3)? The simple answer is that our first cause must be to restore the fear of the Lord in the land. This can only be accomplished if, in humility, we individually and collectively repent of our progressive usurpation of godhood, allowing God to once again become "God."

While in point of fact, God *is* God, we as His creatures must allow Him to *be* God in our lives. We must "Let God be 'God.'" Our fleshly or carnal nature, however, continually grasps for godhood. The apostle Paul identified this characteristic as becoming increasingly pronounced as the tributaries of history and prophecy converge in the world's final surge toward the Second Coming of Christ. He noted to the Church at Rome:

*When they knew God, they glorified him not **as** God, neither were thankful; but became vain in their imaginations, and their foolish heart was darkened.*

Professing themselves to be wise, they became fools... who changed the truth of God into a lie, and worshiped and served the creature more than the Creator...(Rom. 1:21-25).

How then does God again become "God" ...only when we obey Him. And only when we learn that, as "God," He must be obeyed rather than OK'd, do we have any genuine hope of truly loving Him.

Lawlessness is the natural end of the creature elevating him or herself as co-equal to or greater than the Creator. And in these last days we are warned that lawlessness shall increase. The looming Anti-christ will himself be called the "Wicked" or "lawless one" (II Thess. 2:8). Law-lessness occurs progressively and incrementally as God loses His rightful estimation as "God" in our individual, collective, and even church life. When God is no longer truly treated as "God," we have lost the fear of the Lord, and *The Secret of the Lord* escapes our apprehension.

How God Becomes "God"

How then does God again become "God," both in spirit and in truth? He becomes "God" in both spirit and truth only when we obey Him. And only when we learn that, as "God," He must be obeyed rather than OK'd, do we have any genuine hope of truly loving Him. Satan, the enemy of your soul, well knows this to be true, for he was cast out due to his rebellion against God as "God," making himself, in effect, to be equal with God.

This arch Deceiver… seeks to choreograph all creation to declare themselves equal to God by dis-obeying His Word as "God"… His goal is to totally replace the fear of the Lord with the fear of man.

This arch Deceiver of all the earth, from the Garden to Golgotha and now to the edge of eternal Glory, seeks to choreograph all creation to declare themselves equal to God by dis-obeying His Word as "God" (Gen. 3:1-5). His goal is to totally replace the fear of the Lord with the fear of man, ultimately shifting allegiance from God to a man-centered, god-less government, (where hope becomes horror and delight becomes despair) thus eternally severing access to *The Secret of The Lord.*

God becomes "God" in our lives and society only when and as you and I become as little children, first restoring the fear of the Father as "God," not embracing Him as our egalitarian equal. As we restore the genuine fear of the Lord, revealed in child-like obedience in humility of heart, without equivocation, true faith will gradually replace fear as God's favor opens to us in trusting relationship. God then, as truly "God," will embrace us with the yearned-for warmth of His love, and we will know Him truly as *Abba Father* as His promised healing, hope, and yes, Heaven, become a living reality.

FROM FEAR TO FATHER

It should no longer seem a mystery how we have arrived in the spiritual muddle of this generation as we await the soon-return of the Messiah redeemer. For at least three generations, worldly wisdom has worked Satan's nefarious will, turning children told by God to obey their parents into self-glorifying, selfish and spoiled rebels whose true "God" is created in their own image to serve their ever-increasing lust for power, perks, and position as "divine" rights. The emerging picture of this spirit of rebellion can be clearly seen throughout the entire planet, regardless of culture.

Fear of man has now metastasized throughout the earth, supplanting the fear of God.... Men's hearts failing them for fear... looking after those things which are coming on the earth.

Fear of man has now metastasized throughout the earth, supplanting the fear of God. If we do not fear God, we will fear man. Jesus gravely warned of this gripping moment in history. In describing these end times in detail, the Father's "only begotten son" told of terror...

Men's hearts failing them for fear, and for looking after those things which are coming on the earth: for the powers of heaven shall be shaken" (Luke 21:26).

God, knowing the terrifying fear that will grip all of humanity in these days as they continue in rebellion against Him as "God," experiencing the unfolding and unexpected consequences of refusing to fear God as His humble creation, still reaches out His hand to you and to me.

Jesus knew that few would follow. He knew that most would reject the fear of the Lord, choosing rather to fear man. He knew that *The Secret of the Lord* would remain forever "secret" to the vast majority of mankind.

*Because strait is the gate, and narrow is the way, which
leadeth unto life, and few there be that find it.*

*[Yet]…broad is the way, that leadeth to destruction,
and many there be which go in thereat (Matt. 7:13-14).*

It broke Jesus' heart and the Father-heart of God. Not only
pagans but professing believers, both Jew and Gentile, would
refuse to fear God in humble obedience. As Jesus lamented…

*Not every one that saith to me Lord, Lord, shall enter
into the kingdom of heaven; but he that doeth the will
of my Father which is in heaven.*

*Many will say to me in that day, Lord, Lord…and then
will I profess unto them, I never knew you: depart from
me ye that work iniquity.*

The Goddess of Reason

When we do not truly fear God *as* God, we become as co-
participant with workers of iniquity. From God's perspective as
Father of the household of faith, anyone who does not properly *fear* Him *as* Father, acknowledging on every issue of life
and eternity that "Father knows best," is
in reality a rebel and a worker of iniquity.
This was the very iniquity that was found
in Lucifer, causing him to be cast out of
God's presence.

Lucifer had an egalitarian spirit. It
was the same spirit that drove the French
Revolution, resulting in the Reign of
Terror in so-called democratic France.
Lucifer fashioned himself as "equal" with
God, thereby rendering (in his mind) that

*Lucifer had an egali-
tarian spirit. It was
the same spirit that
drove the French
Revolution, resulting
in the Reign of Terror
in so-called demo-
cratic France.*

he need not obey God. The rebel cry of the French Revolution was "Liberty, Equality and Fraternity." The goal was not only to be "equal" among men but to be "equal" to God. And so history records the French as deposing God's genuine authority through Faith and Family, erecting instead the "Goddess of Reason" in the heart of Paris.

The spirit of the French Revolution has become the global fashion du jour. The entire world, including ...professing Christians and many pastors, are in various stages of egalitarian rebellion against the God of Creation.

The spirit of the French Revolution has become the global fashion *du jour.* The entire world, including Gentiles, Jews, professing Christians and many pastors, are in various stages of egalitarian rebellion against the God of Creation. The litmus test of this rebellion is in our arrogant refusal to agree with what God has said in His Word...the Father's word to the household of faith. It is *deja vu.* It is the devastating drama of deception from the Garden of Eden repeating itself in those who profess to be God's "children."

Are we truly God's "children" if we refuse to agree with Him? If we erect in our minds the "Goddess of Reason" to rationalize away...what Father God has said.

But are we truly God's "children" if we refuse to agree with Him? If we erect in our minds the "Goddess of Reason" to rationalize away or dismiss as culturally irrelevant what Father God has said, have we not made ourselves equal with God? And having made ourselves effectively "equal" with God, can we truly say with a straight face that we fear God *as* God? Have we not disqualified ourselves from access to *The Secret of the Lord?*

LOVING OBEDIENCE OPENS LIFE

It is no secret that the word *obey* has become one of the most despised words in the western world, perhaps most notably in the broader Christian church, from Europe to America. So great is the antipathy toward the word *obey*, that it is treated as "a four-letter word" (to use a vernacular expression describing words so on the extreme margin of common cultural acceptability as to be unprintable without public remonstrance).

Obedience, which God says lives at the very heart of a genuine loving relationship between the Creator and those made in His image, has become a matter to be mocked, often eliciting public scorn and private derision, from pulpit to pew. We have even created non-biblical, religious-sounding labels such as "legalism" to justify licentious living under the guise of freely loving God. We can even claim to love the Torah while tacitly rejecting its truth, kissing its scrolls while corrupting its living sanctity.

But consider for a moment the manner in which such "blasphemy" has come to be. Both the source…and the solution…are simple if we see with the eyes of children. A child left to himself to "do his own thing" will persist in ever-more pronounced and obnoxiously selfish behavior unless acted upon by an outside force, i.e., parents or other authority figures. A child must learn obedience, and obedience is learned under the loving law of a father and his wife, where consistency of compliance is clearly expected and enforced.

As the infant transitions into early childhood, the father and mother begin to gradually lay out for the child the pattern of life and purpose in the household as well as the liberties and law that will define relationships. Up to that point of life, the child has done almost everything he or she wants, because it did not seriously impinge upon family relationships, and such expectations would have been unreasonable. Suddenly, the child is faced with limitations to her willful ways. She must now comply with conditions, guidelines and restrictions or face correction. That which the child *wants* to do is now curtailed by what he/she *ought* to do.

This is the crucible in which genuine love of the father or ungodly attitudes of rebellion (which always frustrates relationships) are formed. For this reason, again, children are admonished by God to "obey your parents in the Lord: for this is right" and to "Honour thy father and mother; which is the first commandment with promise" (Eph. 6:1-3). Similarly, fathers are warned to "provoke not your children to wrath…" (Eph. 6:4).

Love is rooted in godly law. A child does not learn to truly love his/her father with authenticity until that child learns to humbly honour and respect the father by obeying the godly laws of the father's household. Obedience breeds trust, and trust breeds greater and more frequent obedience with a growing awareness of increasing warmth of relationship blossoming into love.

There can be no true love of God without obedience.

The more a child comes to perceive the truly "awesome" godly nature and role of his/her father displayed in loving consistency, even in correction, the greater the growth of the child's love and the more willing and complete his obedience.

TRUST and OBEY. There is no other way to be "happy in Jesus." Loving obedience opens life. Loving obedience to the law of God the Father, as re-iterated in the obedient life of Christ, is the narrow way to *The Secret of the Lord*. Obedience is the manner in which we truly reveal the genuine fear of the Lord in our lives.

God's love is unconditional. However, all of the blessings and promises of God are conditional.

Love is first demonstrated in obedience. To obey is better than all of our religiosity and ritual. There can be no true love of God without obedience.

LOVING GOD

God's love is unconditional. However, all of the blessings and promises of God are conditional. They are conditional upon our response.

A father can be ever so loving toward his child, but if the child persists in resisting that father's love and indeed rebels against it, not only will that child fail to experience the joy of fellowship that would have been available but most likely will jeopardize the blessings that otherwise would have been available through the caring compassion of his father. Furthermore, it is in the father's control whether or not the child should receive an inheritance. Love was extended unconditionally, but inheritance is always conditional to the father's will.

So it is with God as Father. God is love, but He looks for responsive evidence of love from those who profess to be His children. That responsive evidence is that we "do his will" and "obey His voice." Jesus, as the "only begotten son" of God, well understood the simplicity of this truth. Repeatedly He said, "My will is to do the will of him that sent me." Jesus, our "elder brother," submitted his own will to that of his Father.

It is said of Jesus that, as a child, he "learned obedience by the things which he suffered" (Heb. 5:8). As a man, the Lord of the Church, the Savior of the World, "humbled himself, and became obedient unto death, even the death of the cross."

Wherefore God also hath highly exalted him, and hath given him a name which is above every name:

That at the name of Jesus every knee should bow…and that every tongue should confess that Jesus Christ is Lord…(Phil. 2:8-11).

That same Jesus, exalted by God the Father because of his humble obedience on earth, beckons you and me to open the treasure chest of truth through discovery of *The Secret of the Lord* in the very same manner. As the Son obeyed the Father without sin or rebellion, even so we are to obey the Son, as the "only-begotten Son," so that we might "receive the adoption of sons" through Jesus Christ (Gal. 4:4). All, whether Jew or Gentile, who embrace Messiah's sacrifice of himself as the Lamb of God and who walk in obedience and repentance, are "grafted in" to the original olive tree of Israel. In Christ they have become "the Israel of God" (Rom. 11; Rom. 2:28-29), "heirs according to the promise."

Jesus said "I and the Father are one." "He that hath seen me hath seen the Father" (Jn. 14:9). To lovingly obey Jesus is to lovingly obey and conform to the Father's will. Therefore Jesus was explicit in how to love God.

If you love me, keep my commandments (Jn. 14:15).

He that hath my commandments, and keepeth them, he it is that loveth me: and he that loveth me shall be loved of my Father, and I will love him, and will manifest myself to him (Jn. 14:21).

If a man love me, he will keep my words: and my Father will love him, and we will come unto him, and make our abode with him (Jn. 4:23).

He that loveth me not, keepeth not my sayings: and the word that ye hear is not mine, but the Father's which sent me (Jn. 14:24).

Jesus' beloved disciple, John, having known Jesus in close fellowship, re-enforced the power and necessity of obedience in truly loving God and in experiencing His love.

For this is the love of God, that we keep his commandments: and his commandments are not grievous (I Jn. 5:1).

By this we know that we love the children of God, when we love God, and keep his commandments (I Jn. 5:2).

He that keepeth his commandments dwelleth in him, and he in him (I Jn. 3:24).

And this is love, that we walk after his commandments (II Jn. 6).

LOVING GOD'S WORD

Most people believe in God. Approximately 90 percent of Americans claim to believe IN God. Most of the 7 billion people on the planet believe in a god or gods of some type. Even the devil and his demonic host believe in God (Jam. 2:19). Yet there is a profound difference between Satan's belief in God and the belief of most who claim to be "spiritual"...including the belief of most modern and post-modern professing Christians. The difference is dramatic and has the potential to determine eternal destiny.

The Bible declares that the devils "believe and tremble" (Jam. 2:19). They actually *tremble* before God and His Word. But why? Demonic spirits seem to have greater spiritual discernment than do democratically-dominated Christians in this last-days generation. The devils not only believe but actually tremble. Yet the very thought of trembling before God or His Word today is virtually taboo, from pulpit to pew. We have not only lost but have affirmatively abandoned the fear of the Lord. God has, in effect, become our egalitarian equal. And a person, whether pastor, priest, rabbi or parishioner, finds no purpose in trembling in the presence of his/her equal.

Yet God is still "God." Yes, He loves us, even as a "Father," but He is not our equal, nor does He take pleasure in our perception that He is nothing more than the operator of a heavenly slot machine to dispense good fortune because we claim *faith* while arrogantly refusing to *fear* Him. "I am the Lord, and there is none else, there is no God beside me" declares the Creator (Isa. 45:5-6).

Ultimately, we know we *fear* the Lord when we *tremble* at His Word. When Father speaks, the true children listen and obey. For Yeshua Messiah said, "My sheep hear my voice, and I know them, and they follow me" (Jn. 10:27). "To this man will I look," saith the Lord, "even to him that is poor and of a contrite spirit, and *trembleth* at my word" (Isa. 66:2).

> *Ultimately, we know we fear the Lord when we tremble at His Word.*

If I do not tremble at the Word of God, I do not truly fear God. He is not truly my Father and I may well not truly be of His household of faith, notwithstanding all my confessions and protestations to the contrary. It is not that I can earn salvation by conjuring fear of God in my mind by faith. Rather, the lack of genuine reverent fear of God and His Word reveals I have not yet come to the moment of truth where I see God *as* God and myself as eternally separated from His holiness by my own sin...that but for His goodness that leads me to repentance, I am without hope both in this world and in the world to come (Rom. 2:3-4).

Therefore, if I would truly love God, I must first learn to tremble in His presence and at His Word. Both God and His Word must be embraced in the awesome understanding that when God has spoken, man cannot and must not seek to diminish or modify by adding to, taking away from, rationalizing or "spinning" the supremacy of Scripture to accommodate his whims or opposing cultural notions.

> *This sense of the absolute divine authority of God and His Word has nearly disappeared from our consciousness and culture.*

This sense of the absolute divine authority of God and His Word has nearly disappeared from our consciousness and culture. When less than 50 percent of professing Christians in America claim to believe in absolute truth, we are truly in trouble. But when only 9 percent of professing Christian young people embrace anything approaching absolute truth, any true faith in God *as* God has been and will continue to be supplanted by the authoritative demands of fleeting feelings, leading not to love of God and His Word but to "spiritualized" licentiousness.

The genuine fear of the Lord and a trembling at His Word as the Word of the King of kings and Lord of lords is the only pathway to loving God and His Word. Just as an infant, upon entering early childhood, must learn first to honor and respect the word and authority of his/her father as the avenue to a mature love, so it is with our spiritual lives. If the God-defined and disclosed pattern is altered so as to try to expedite maturity, the parent-child relationship will become distorted with serious discipline problems resulting. Rebellion will vie for authority against righteous relationship, which we clearly see revealing its ugly head throughout America and the western world.

As with the natural relationship between parent and child, so it is with the supernatural relationship between humankind and "Father" God. We have effectively erected a spiritual "Berlin Wall" to frustrate access to *The Secret of the Lord*. That access will only be recovered to this generation as we individually and corporately confess to and repent of our childish usurpation of God's authority and, in profound humility, embrace God *as* God, thereby progressively restoring a true love both for God and His inerrant Word.

If we make the choice, God, by His grace and in His mercy, will help us make the change. But time is short.

Chapter 14

PROVOCATIVE THOUGHTS FOR
SECRET SEEKERS

1. Why is it necessary to strongly re-assert that God is "GOD?"

2. What happens when we drift away from treating God as "GOD?"

3. How does God become "GOD" again in our lives?

4. Do you agree that we, like those in the French Revolution, have effectively erected "The Goddess of Reason" in our lives, even as professing Christians?

5. Have you been inclined to resist the word *obey* in your life? Why?

6. What is the difference between believing IN God and actually BELIEVING God?

7. Do you "tremble" at the Word of the Lord? Why...or why not? How does this relate to the *fear of the Lord* and to gaining access to *The SECRET of the Lord?*

CHAPTER 15

Finding "Perfect Love"

*"If ye will fear the Lord, and serve Him, and obey
His voice and not rebel…then shall both ye and also
the king that reigneth over you continue following
the Lord your God" (II Sam. 12:14).*

"PERFECT LOVE CASTETH OUT FEAR," DECLARED JESUS'
"beloved disciple," John (I Jn. 4:18). And who among us does
not want a "perfect love" that would remove fear? "Fear has torment," observed the apostle John, but does the fear of the Lord
have "torment?" It might, depending upon how we respond
to or reject God's love. But in this chapter, we need to explore
how "perfect love casts out fear."

TWO TYPES OF FEAR

If indeed the Word of God expects and even commands us
to fear God, how then can the same divinely-inspired Scriptures
declare, "There is no fear in love" (I Jn. 4:18)? The answer is relatively simple to state, yet relatively difficult to live out because

of our human or carnal, fleshly nature that continually seeks to bring God into submission to our will.

First, there are two basic types of fear that we face. When we say we are "fearful" or are "dealing with fear," we are most likely referring to some object, development, person, authority, whether actual or potential, that causes us to be afraid in protection of life, limb or some life purpose or principle, whether for ourselves or others. The reason we are afraid is because we inherently sense our well-being is threatened by some outside force over which we may have little or no control. The greater the sense of inability to control combined with exposure to perceived risk, the greater the fear.

There is a second type of fear, however, that has been the primary thrust of our journey toward discovering *The Secret of the Lord.* This fear is not so much focused on the emotional reaction of being afraid, but rather on the profound nature, character and authority of someone with whom we have association...especially the Creator of the universe. If great leaders find themselves awestruck, spellbound and intimidated in the presence of the President of the United States, what infinitely greater *fear* or profound and humbling respect should bring us to our knees in the presence of a holy God?

The greater the love, the less the intimidating fear that frustrates growing relationship. So it is in our relationship with God.

The less the relationship with such power or authority, the greater the "fear," the sense of separation and feeling of absolute intimidation. The greater the relationship, the more likely it becomes that intimidation fades into a kind of intimacy while profound respect is preserved. The greater the love, the less the intimidating fear that frustrates growing relationship.

So it is in our relationship with God. While not diminishing the awesome honor and respect that His very Being demands and commands, perfecting our love for Him, in obedience, progressively "casteth out fear." As intimidating fear is supplanted by a holy love, in full cognizance that God is still "God," the passageway to *The Secret of the Lord* is made accessible. There is no alternative way.

NO FEAR IN LOVE

"There is no fear in love; but perfect love casteth out fear. He that feareth is not made perfect in love" (I Jn. 4:18). Here is the true test of our trust…perfect love. It begins with our profound sense of God's unmatched majesty and glory and ends with His allowing just a bit of His reflected glory to be seen in and through our lives. It begins with the hand of un-matched majesty being extended to man in divine love and progresses to our loving response to such magnanimity with joyful obedience.

"Perfect love casteth out fear." It casts out the terror we may rightly experience contemplating the absolute holiness of God in the face of our abject unrighteousness.

Indeed, "perfect love casteth out fear." It casts out the terror we may rightly experience contemplating the absolute holiness of God in the face of our abject unrighteousness. For "fear hath torment" (I Jn. 4:18). But God, yearning as a Father for restored fellowship with you and me, is unwilling to leave us in a place of torment, without our willful choice. His goodness leads us to repentance and restored relationship, replacing unholy and paralyzing fear with a holy life promising joyful fellowship.

This is the Father's plan and purpose. "For God so loved the world, that he gave his only begotten Son, that whosoever believeth on him [accepts, embraces Jesus as Savior and Messiah…the only way, truth and life, repents of sin, and joyfully walks in obedience and a holy lifestyle] should not perish but have everlasting life" (Jn. 3:16).

Whether you have never committed your life to Jesus Christ in this way or whether you once did but have forgotten or fled from your first love, this is your moment of surrender to His lordship. "Today, if you will hear His voice, harden not your heart" (Heb. 3:7-8, 15). Time is short.

FEAR HAS TORMENT

As human beings, we want so badly to embrace God as a God of *love*, that we tend to tacitly (or even intentionally) reject Him as a God of truth and judgment. The God of the Bible is not an "either/or" God but rather a "both/and" God. He is both love and truth. Therefore Jesus, God in the flesh, is both love and truth, both mercy and the ultimate judge (Jn. 5:22, 26-27; Rom. 2:16). "We beheld his glory," noted John, "full of [both] grace and truth" (Jn. 1:14).

> *As human beings, we want so badly to embrace God as a God of love, that we tend to tacitly...reject Him as a God of truth and judgment.*

Our rebellious carnal natures warmly embrace the God of love but are coldly repelled by the God of truth. Rebels always reject truth, but they rejoice in someone they perceive will accept them in their lawless state without requiring change to pursue relationship. This persistent state of lawless rebellion against God as "Truth" has, for two generations, led to our need for a divine "makeover," thus re-imagining or reconstructing God in our image. We demand a God who will receive us into His holy embrace without repentance... without conforming to His will. An absolute God who is absolute truth is now absolutely unacceptable, even among professing Christians.

> *Rebels always reject truth, but they rejoice in someone they perceive will accept them in their lawless state without requiring change to pursue relationship.*

Having thus disrespected God as "God," we find ourselves in a very difficult position. We must either find or create a way to justify our rebellious disagreement with God and His Word, or we must humbly admit our lawless disagreement (whether in spirit or truth, whether in theology or behavior) and repent, confessing our sin, changing our ways, and being restored to relational favor.

We demand a God who will receive us into His holy embrace without repentance… without conforming to His will.

The persistent Holy Spirit, the "spirit of truth," will not allow us to linger long in spiritual limbo without bringing conviction to mind and heart. When conviction of broken relationship comes, we must quickly respond to that gentle but persistent voice. Delay can be dangerous, leading to self-deception and self-justification, thus further separating us from the God we claim to love and serve.

Rejection of God's grace and kindness through the loving conviction of His Spirit leads inevitably to condemnation. If we are not walking according to the Spirit, we are necessarily walking according to our flesh, giving Satan place to will and to do of his good pleasure. Favor with God is replaced by a new aspect of fear. God calls it "torment." As the apostle John clearly warned, "fear hath torment" (I Jn. 4:18).

The persistent Holy Spirit, the "spirit of truth," will not allow us to linger long in spiritual limbo without bringing conviction to mind and heart. We must quickly respond to that gentle but persistent voice. Delay can be dangerous, leading to self-deception and self-justification, thus further separating us from the God we claim to love and serve.

We are "tormented" in our mind, heart and spirit, because we are made spiritual beings in God's image but are living, by choice, outside of His favor and the ways of His family. That is neither a pleasant nor peaceful place to be. It has torment. We are troubled, and that spiritual dis-equilibrium echoes throughout every aspect of our lives, relationships, decisions and even in our physical and spiritual health.

"Fear hath torment!" That torment, whether seemingly passive or persistent, constant or recurring, is directly related to God as "truth." Truth requires justice and judgment. And it is the ultimate fear of judgment by a holy God that can tyrannize our lives.

Fear of judgment is both good and godly when seen as the ultimate consequence of our refusal to humbly yield to God's convicting kindness which is prodding us to repentance so that our relationship might be restored. As we respond in simple, repentant, child-like faith, terror is replaced by a new, restored and refreshing love of the truth. If I do not love God's truth and the God of truth, I am under judgment, condemnation and torment.

We cannot sing, "O, How I Love Jesus," and not love Jesus as the Truth, who came to bear witness to the truth, and who will judge all men according to the Truth. For it is the Truth and only the Truth that will "make us free" (Jn. 8:32).

*Wherefore we receiving a kingdom that cannot be moved, let us have grace, whereby we may serve God acceptably with **reverence** and godly fear: For our God is a consuming fire (Heb. 12:28-29).*

CASTING OUT FEAR

Let us remember, then, that "perfect love casteth out fear." "He that feareth is not made perfect in love" (I Jn. 4:18).

"If a man say, I love God, and hateth his brother, he is a liar: for he that loveth not his brother whom he hath seen, how can he love God whom he hath not seen?" "He who loveth God loveth his brother also" (I Jn. 4:20-21).

"God is love; and he that dwelleth in love dwelleth in God, and God in him" (I Jn. 4:16). "This is the love of God, that we keep his commandments: and his commandments are not grievous" (I Jn. 5:3).

"We must all appear before the judgment seat of Christ; that every one may receive the things done in his body, according to that he hath done, whether it be good or bad. Knowing therefore the terror of the Lord, we persuade men (II Cor. 5:10-11).

"Herein is our love made perfect, that we may have boldness in the day of judgment: because as he is, so are we in this world" (I Jn. 4:17). Jesus, as "the Word made flesh," obeyed God fully as a man in the earth. He was the "last Adam," restoring hope for eternal life by His loving obedience to the Father, "full of grace and truth" (Jn. 1:14). Christ so lived and died in obedience that he might "deliver them who through fear of death were all their lifetime subject to bondage" (Heb. 2:15).

Loving obedience casts out fear. There is no torment in loving obedience…only peace.

Loving obedience casts out fear. There is no torment in loving obedience…only peace. But the wrath of God abides on those who both refuse to believe and who refuse to obey (Jn. 3:36, Rom. 1:18, Col. 3:6). Therefore, "Let no man deceive you with vain words: for because of these things cometh the wrath of God upon the children of disobedience" (Eph. 5:6).

"Be ye therefore followers of God as dear children; and walk in love…" (Eph. 5:1). But "Be not deceived: neither fornicators, nor idolaters, nor adulterers, nor effeminate, nor abusers of themselves with mankind, nor thieves, nor covetous, nor drunkards, nor revilers, nor extortioners shall inherit the kingdom of God." "Know ye not that the unrighteous shall not inherit the kingdom of God" (I Cor. 6:9-10)?

Therefore, as Jesus said, "Repent: for the kingdom of heaven is at hand" (Matt. 4:17). "Because strait is the gate, and narrow is the way, which leadeth unto life [*The Secret of the Lord*], and few there be that find it" (Matt. 7:14).

Chapter 15

PROVOCATIVE THOUGHTS FOR
SECRET SEEKERS

1. If "there is no fear in love," why then are we to fear God?

2. Why are we so prone to either reject or run from the *fear of the Lord?*

3. Why is "fear of judgment" both good and godly?

4. What ultimately "casts out fear" in our lives?

5. Will you "have boldness" in the day of judgment? Why...or why not?

Unveiling the Secret

"Fear the Lord, and serve Him in truth with all your heart: for consider how great things He hath done for you" (I Sam. 12:24).

THE FINAL CURTAIN OF THE DIVINE DRAMA OF HIStory is ready to be drawn. The stage has been set, and expectations of the final ACT are drawing the imagination of mankind worldwide. Timing is deemed to be critical, and tensions are mounting.

Will there truly be a messiah? When will He make His appearance? How will we know? Will there truly be an imposter, a counterfeit masquerading as messiah to deceive the global audience? How can I best prepare for prophesied events that will strike unprecedented terror upon terra firma, this earth we call *home*?

The Bible, God's Word, which is also His love letter to mankind, makes plain His purposes for these dramatic times. It is time to rivet our attention lest the unveiling of *The Secret of the Lord* somehow escape our comprehension amid the tumult of our times.

TRIBULATION BRINGS TERROR

God has warned us. Terror is coming upon the earth. Terrorism has been sweeping the globe, drawing the attention and defenses of leaders worldwide. Yet these expressions of terror are merely a scattered premonition of that which will soon become universally prominent. Intervening in this final historical ACT will be a breath of false peace presented by a counterfeit "Prince of Peace" which the Scriptures call the "Wicked" or "Lawless One," the "son of perdition" (II Thess. 2:3-8).

This imposter "messiah" will be exceedingly crafty and deceptive. His work and ways will be as deceptive as those of the arch Deceiver, Satan, whose final war against the God of Creation will be waged in all-out craftiness against those created in God's image. No holds will be barred. It will be the final battle to determine the eternal destiny of all then living. And fear will be the final driving force to propel the majority of mankind into the "broad way" that leads to destruction (Matt. 7:13).

Satan...has designed his most effective weapon for your destruction. If he cannot capture your commitment to his cause through deception, he will do so through fear. Fear and terror are his tried and true tools.

Satan is determined. He has designed his most effective weapon for your destruction. If he cannot capture your commitment to his cause through deception, he will do so through fear. Fear and terror are his tried and true tools. He is calculating your final capitulation, especially for Israel and for those who confess Christ as savior, to follow his pernicious ways in fear.

The Destroyer, fallen Lucifer, has raised up a man who, like Satan, "shall magnify himself in his heart," and purporting to be the awaited "prince of peace," will "stand up against the Prince of princes," the true Messiah and prophesied "Prince of Peace" (Dan. 8:23-25, Isa. 9:6-7). Through the pursuit of peace, he "shall destroy many," especially the physical and spiritual descendants of Abraham, Isaac and Jacob, whether Jew or Gentile (Dan. 8:23-24). The prophet Daniel explicitly foretold that this will happen, "in the latter time" (Dan. 8:23). And these are those long-awaited times.

Truth Combats Terror

Truth does not deny terror but destroys it. One ounce of truth can dispel a mighty onslaught of terror. It is not the truth itself, but rather our embracing and fully yielding our body, soul and spirit to God's truth that puts fear to flight. Just as a little light dispels darkness, even so God's truth, believed and acted upon by those who fear Him, dispels the otherwise terrifying darkness that is rapidly enveloping the earth. *The Secret of the Lord* is that foundational, terror and fear-dispelling, truth that must be unveiled. The time for the unveiling is now.

Just as a little light dispels darkness, even so God's truth, believed and acted upon by those who fear Him, dispels the otherwise terrifying darkness that is rapidly enveloping the earth. The Secret of the Lord is that foundational, fear-dispelling, truth.

The Day of The Lord

The Scriptures repeatedly, in both the Tanakh (Old Testament) and in the New Testament, solemnly warn of a period in "the latter days" called "the day of the Lord" (Joel 2:1-11, Zeph. 1:14-18, Zech. 14:1, Amos 5:18, II Pet. 3:10, I Thess. 5:2). Sometimes it is referred to as "the day of Christ" (II Thess. 2:2), or from a Jewish perspective, "the day of the Messiah."

The expectation of a soon-coming Messiah is growing month-by-month across the globe. Even pagans, unbelievers and disbelievers and those of religions other than Christianity are speaking openly of their sense that something beyond anything heretofore experienced in the annals of history is about to be manifested. It is truly an amazing phenomena sweeping the earth.

World leaders dare not openly discuss this "day of darkness" (Amos 5:18, Joel 2:2), fearing political disaster and global uprising. This growing political instability coupled with economic upheaval is even now ushering in a new global order in which mankind's hard-fought freedoms are being offered up as a sacrifice on the altar of false promises of "peace and security," "security and prosperity," or what the physical descendants of Abraham, Isaac and Jacob call "Shalom." Yet, as we have noted from Daniel's prophecy, many will be destroyed through this false pursuit of peace (Dan. 8:25).

"Be not soon shaken in mind, or be troubled…as that the day of Christ is at hand," exhorted the apostle Paul to the Church at Thessalonica (II Thess. 2:2). Yet, said Paul, "the day of the Lord so cometh as a thief in the night." "For when they shall say, Peace and safety; then sudden destruction cometh upon them…." "But ye, brethren, [speaking to true believers and disciples of Jesus as Messiah] are not in darkness, that that day should overtake you as a thief" (I Thess. 5:2-4). "Let us not sleep, as do others, but let us watch and be sober [serious minded]" (I Thess. 5:6).

FIGHTING FEAR BY FAITH

"But let us, who are of the day, be sober [serious minded], putting on the breastplate of faith and love; and for an helmet, the hope of salvation," enjoined Paul. "Wherefore comfort yourselves together, and edify one another…" (I Thess. 5:11).

Again, writes Paul, "For the Lord himself shall descend from heaven with a shout, with the voice of the archangel, and with the trump of God: and the dead in Christ [true believers in Yeshua who have died] shall rise first: Then we which are alive and remain shall be caught up [raptured] together with them in the clouds to meet the Lord in the air: and so shall we ever be with the Lord. Wherefore, comfort one another with these words" (I Thess. 4:16-18).

For many, these words strike terror rather than comfort. Whether these words strike fear or comfort depends solely upon your relationship with your Creator, with Jesus Christ, the Savior of the world. True faith, lived out in righteous obedience and repentance, will leave fear famished. Fear will have nothing to feed upon. Terror will not triumph over truth deeply embedded in your mind and heart. "This is the victory that overcometh the world, even our faith" (I Jn. 5:4).

True faith, lived out in righteous obedience and repentance, will leave fear famished…. Terror will not triumph over truth deeply embedded in your mind and heart.

Why, then, will vast numbers of professing believers in Jesus fall away amid the growing fear, terror and pressure [tribulations] of the last days before Christ appears (II Thess. 2:3, II Tim. 4:3, I Tim. 4:1, II Pet. 2:1-22)? It is because their faith is not complete. They are wide open to deception and wither in the face of daunting fear, because their faith is rooted in their feelings rather than in the truth that will both make and keep them free from fear. They perish, "because they receive not the love of the truth, that they might be saved." "That they all might be damned who believed not the truth, but have pleasure in unrighteousness" (II Thess. 2:10-12).

Why…will vast numbers of professing believers in Jesus fall away amid the growing fear, terror and pressure of the last days before Christ appears? It is because…their faith is rooted in their feelings rather than in the truth.

This is not a time for theological debate but for true belief revealed in steadfast love of Christ, who is the Truth, revealed in and through humble obedience and a repentant heart. Theological quibbling and spiritual gymnastics will protect none in the face of the assault of fear increasingly confronting those who profess the name of Christ worldwide. Persecution is rising publically and severely against the saints in virtually every nation on the planet, looking increasingly like the ravages of ancient Rome against those who would publically follow Christ in simple faith.

> *Fear is vanquished as we live by faith…. Faith is not just something we have, but is something we do.*

"God hath not given us the spirit of fear," reminded Paul, "but of power, and of love, and of a sound mind" (II Tim. 1:7). This is not just a generalized concept but is a dependable life-orienting, fear-measuring truth. If God has not given me this fear that increasingly terrorizes my mind, threatening to paralyze my life and decisions, then what is its source? The answer should be clear. I have given permission to my fleshly nature to be progressively and systematically overtaken by Satan's ultimate weapon. In so "giving place to the Devil," I have frustrated the grace of God given to enable me to face, by faith, every onslaught brought against me. Rather than being a victor, I have voluntarily made myself a victim.

> *Fear can only be fought by faith. And genuine, operative faith finds its fulcrum in the fear of the Lord. We must recover the fear of the Lord to release The Secret of the Lord for the increasingly troubling and trying times that are coming, when men's hearts will fail them for fear, because the very "powers of heaven shall be shaken."*

It is written, "The just shall live by his faith" (Hab. 2:4, Rom. 4:3). Fear is vanquished as we live by faith. Notice! Faith is not just something we *have*, but is something we *do*. Belief always requires corresponding behavior to validate the reality of that which we say we believe. And never is that behavioral validation more needed and revealed than when we are confronted with intimidating, life-threatening fear of men's power, position, or persuasion that puts at risk our very person and destiny.

Fear can only be fought by faith. And genuine, operative faith finds its fulcrum in the fear of the Lord. We must recover the fear of the Lord to release *The Secret of the Lord* for the increasingly troubling and trying times that are coming, when men's hearts will fail them for fear, because the very "powers of heaven shall be shaken" (Luke 21:26).

Would those who witness your life at home, in your neighborhood, in the gym or in your place of work be able to testify beyond a reasonable doubt that you truly fear the Lord? What does the witness of your own heart disclose in the innermost recesses of your mind? If doubt prevails or lurks in the shadowed recesses of your mind and conscience, there is persuasive evidence that you are prone to fear man rather than God.

The next chapters will reveal in stark reality the eternal significance of recovering the fear of the Lord, for in truth, we will either fear God…or man. *The Secret of the Lord* lies on the other side of our decision.

Chapter 16

PROVOCATIVE THOUGHTS FOR SECRET SEEKERS

1. In what ways are *fear* and *terror* Satan's tried and tested tools?

2. How does *truth* dispel terror?

3. What will be the driving force to propel the majority of mankind to spiritual destruction?

4. Why do you think there is a growing "messianic" expectation throughout the earth?

5. How can you fight fear through faith?

CHAPTER 17

History's Final Act

"As the heaven is high above the earth, so great is His mercy toward them that fear Him" (Psa. 103:11).

WE WILL EITHER FEAR GOD, OR MAN. THERE REMAIN no other options. Mankind stands now at his/her moment of truth in the valley of decision. Will we fear God...or man? Destiny rides in the balance.

THE BEGINNING OF WISDOM

We well know from God's viewpoint the most basic of all spiritual truth:

The fear of the Lord is the beginning of wisdom: and the knowledge of the holy is understanding (Prov. 9:10).

If "the fear of the Lord" is the "beginning" of wisdom, what might be wisdom's final expression? In this chapter, we will soon discover the amazing ribbon of connectivity between God's communication of what He deemed of foundational importance under the Tanakh or Old Covenant and what remains of ultimate importance just before *History's Final Act* in the New Covenant.

WHY GOD CARES

God wants you to discover His secret. He has declared His secret to be "secret" precisely because He wants us to seek it out and find it. Indeed, says the Lord,

Not only does God want us to seek Him, but He assures us we will find Him…IF… we search for Him with our whole heart. That search begins with the fear of the Lord…the beginning of all true wisdom.

Ye shall seek me, and find me, when ye shall search for me with your whole heart. And I will be found of you, saith the Lord (Jer. 29:13-14).

What a tremendous and comforting promise. Not only does God want us to seek Him, but He assures us we will find Him…IF…we search for Him with our whole heart. That search begins with the fear of the Lord which is the beginning of all true wisdom, as God, our Creator, sees it. This may seem a bit repetitive, but it is an absolute requirement to discovering *The Secret of the Lord*. The "fear of the Lord" is at the head of the only life trail that leads to discovery of His *secret*.

The "fear of the Lord" is at the head of the only life trail that leads to discovery of His secret.

The problem is that most people do not desire to take that trail. They want the benefits of "the secret" without the perceived burden of the trail that leads to the "secret," indeed to a life-changing, destiny-determining relationship with the Creator of the Universe, the God of the Bible.

God is love. Because He is love, He has not only provided a way but urges us to *find* the way and to search for it "with all your heart." He knows that His *secret* is of utmost significance and must be diligently sought because of the rabbit trails of life that lead everywhere but to His *secret*. That *secret* is the ultimate goal of life from God's viewpoint. It is, from God's perspective, identical with life itself. Discovery of the *secret* and embracing it fully is to "choose life."

> *God is love.... He knows that His secret is of utmost significance and must be diligently sought because of the rabbit trails of life that lead everywhere but to His secret. That secret is the ultimate goal of life from God's viewpoint.*

This was God's message to the Hebrew slaves whom He freed from the bondage of Egypt after 400 years of captivity. "Choose life," He urged, "that both thou and thy seed may live" (Deut. 30:19). Yet they were already alive. They had fled Pharaoh's forces, faced the Red Sea, and forged across on dry land as God led them by the prophetic hand of Moses, yet God told them to "Choose life." They were "alive" in the flesh but had no spiritual life. That is the condition of most, whether pagan, Jew and even professing Christian, as we face "History's Final Act." "Choose life," He urges, "that both thou and thy seed may life."

The choice is ours to make. If we make the choice, God, by His grace, will help us make the necessary changes required to walk the trail toward His "secret." The time to choose is Today, because time is drawing short. "History's Final Act" is unfolding.

No Respecter of Persons

God is not a respecter of persons, but He *is* a respecter of personal choices. Because God is a God of love, He gives us free will to either receive or reject His offer of reconciliation, relationship and redemption. Because God is also a God of truth and justice, there are clear consequences that flow when we receive or reject His Word, His will and His ways.

The apostle Peter was confronted with this simple truth. God had to pull away the restrictive blinders from his spiritual eyes so that he could clearly see God's heart toward all of those created in His image. Peter, raised as a Jew, was convinced that only Jews could truly have favor with God and thereby have access to *The Secret of the Lord*. God, through a vision recorded in Acts 10, convinced Peter otherwise. God, by His Spirit, directed Cornelius, a Roman centurion, to seek out *The Secret of the Lord* from Peter, and because Cornelius sought God sincerely, in spirit and in truth, God began to unveil His "secret" to a gentile centurion. The Jewish Peter was shocked. His response is of profound significance to each of us today.

Those who truly "fear" God are open and available for God's acceptance into relationship out of which His secret begins to be revealed. Those who do not fear God cannot be accepted by God.

> *Of a truth I perceive that God is no respecter of persons:*
> *But in every nation **he that feareth him**, and **worketh***
> ***righteousness**, is accepted with him (Acts 10: 34-35).*

The message is clear. Those who truly "fear" God are open and available for God's acceptance into relationship out of which His secret begins to be revealed. Those who do not fear God cannot be accepted by God.

Secondly, the most elemental evidence of whether or not a person fears God is whether or not the person "worketh righteousness" in alignment with God's Word, will and ways. It is not that a person's works "save" him but rather that the works of right-ways-ness reveal his fundamental attitude and disposition toward God, providing the necessary environment of heart in which the seed of salvation can be planted, yielding the fruit of the unfolding "secret" that has otherwise remained elusive.

Thus, *The Secret of the Lord* is available to every person in every nation, with the sole restriction that anyone who would expect or hope to find the "secret" must fear God as Creator and worship Him as the Maker of heaven and earth by conforming his ways to the ways of his Maker and by being a "worker of righteousness" (Acts 10:35).

> *The Secret of the Lord is of supreme value. Satan, the Deceiver of the whole world, is therefore intent on counterfeiting "the secret" so that human-kind…accepts a cheap substitute promising temporal satisfaction.*

The Coming Counterfeit

Mankind inevitably seeks to counterfeit that which is deemed of considerable value. And *The Secret of the Lord* is of supreme value. Satan, the Deceiver of the whole world, is therefore intent on counterfeiting "the secret" so that humankind cease seeking, accepting a cheap substitute promising temporal satisfaction. This conspiracy to counterfeit, deceiving by offering "False Secrets," was introduced in an earlier chapter. It is time, now, for the rest of the story as we enter *History's Final Act.*

It has been said that "That which is obtained too cheaply is esteemed too lightly." Indeed it is true, yet it never seems to stall man's yearning for cheap substitutes. Satan, the Deceiver, stands ready, able and all too willing to please our fleshly nature. And the Destroyer is rapidly preparing, even now, his ultimate plan to deprive all living of access to *The Secret of the*

> *The Destroyer is rapidly preparing, even now, his ultimate plan to deprive all living of access to* The Secret of the Lord.

Lord. The counterfeit is coming. It is just around the next corner as "History's Final Act" unfolds.

SECURITY AND PROSPERITY

We have seen it before, but must visit it again. The theme defining the rising tide of geo-political restructuring of the globe is "Security and Prosperity" or "Peace and Prosperity." This is Satan's counterfeit promise to *The Secret of the Lord.* Since the planet has largely rejected God's gracious offer of His own "secret," Satan is preparing to woo and wow the world with his own. It will be massive and seemingly miraculous. It will be awe-inspiring, yet driven by fear. It will spiritually seduce by means of fleshly pressure, depriving the desperate masses of all hope of discovering God's "secret" by embracing His arch enemy's clever counterfeit.

The regional governmental power enclaves of the world are now coalescing as prophesied by Daniel for "the latter times" (Dan. 7). Out of this resurrected "Babylonian" global government will arise Satan's counterfeit Christ, "having eyes like a man, and a mouth speaking great [pompous] things" (Dan. 7:8). This usurper of Christ's authority will "speak great words against the Most High [God], and shall wear out [persecute] the saints of the Most High…and they shall be given into his hand until a time and times and the dividing of time [3 ½ years] (Dan. 7:25). He shall "by peace [or the pursuit of peace] destroy many" (Dan. 8:25).

This counterfeit "prince of peace" will seek to achieve his global promise of *Security and Prosperity* through desperate, devious and demonic power, compelling every man, woman and child to wonder after and indeed worship him (Rev. 13:1-7). Indeed, the Bible warns that "all that dwell upon the earth shall worship him, whose names are not written in the book of life of the Lamb [Jesus, Yeshua Messiah] (Rev. 13:8).

Satan does not want your name or any one else's name "written in the book of life of the Lamb," for it is the threshold of the doorway accessing the fulness of *The Secret of the Lord*. The Devil has been eternally deprived of the "secret" and is therefore desperate to deprive all those made in the image of God of access to "the secret." He will seek either to prevent your name from being entered in the "book of life" or to have your name blotted out (Rev. 3:5). His goal is to seduce all to have their names written "in the earth" rather than in heaven (Jer. 17:13).

> *The Devil has been eternally deprived of the "secret" and is therefore desperate to deprive all those made in the image of God of access to "the secret."*

FEAR NEUTRALIZES FAITH

Fear is Satan's ultimate and final weapon to neutralize the remaining vestiges of Biblical faith immediately preceding the Messiah's Second Coming. Fear is an equal-opportunity destroyer. And the enemy of your soul does not play fair. He intends to ruthlessly intimidate mankind through fear, fear of lack of security and prosperity and fear of death, in order to eternally deprive all of access to *The Secret of the Lord*.

Satan's methodology is sure. It has been tried and tested throughout history. Fear tyrannizes faith. As faith wanes, fear wins. The greater the dominion we give to our flesh, the lower the dominance of faith in our spirit. For this reason we are admonished, through the Spirit, to "mortify [put to death] the deeds of the body" so that "ye shall live," because "if we live after the flesh [under its dominion], ye shall die" (Rom. 8:13).

> *Fear is an equal-opportunity destroyer. …The enemy of your soul…intends to ruthlessly intimidate mankind through fear, fear of lack of security and prosperity and fear of death, in order to eternally deprive all of access to The Secret of the Lord.*

THE SECRET OF THE LORD

The Scriptures make plain that Christ, the Messiah, through His death, destroyed the devil's devices which had power through death. Jesus "delivered them who through fear of death were all their lifetime subject to bondage" (Heb. 2:14-15). When fear of physical death looms over our faith, we give back authority to Satan to bring us back into bondage. It is a bondage brokered by fear of death, and it will, unchecked, not only emasculate our faith but ultimately bring us defenseless into carnal covenant with the enemy of our souls, leading to eternal damnation.

SATAN'S SECRET SEDUCTION

Are you prepared to face Satan's final assault against your faith in Jesus Christ? Are you aware of the Devil's design to intimidate the entire world to worship him through fear of death and through temporal promise of earthly provision if only you will pledge your allegiance to his coming kingdom? His design is awaiting your decision. His purpose is pernicious and his plan has been made plain through prophecy. *The Secret of the Lord* is on the line.

The Devil, God's arch enemy, has determined to deceive the entire world...to decimate any remaining vestiges of faith in Yeshua the Messiah... to destroy all hope... to experience the ultimate Secret of the Lord. He is desperate! He is determined! And his time is short.

The Devil, God's arch enemy, has determined to deceive the entire world (Rom. 12:9) in order to decimate any remaining vestiges of faith in Yeshua the Messiah, and to destroy all hope of any denizens of earth to experience the ultimate *Secret of the Lord*. He is desperate! He is determined! And his time is short.

Seduction is Satan's specialized weapon to wage war against the world, especially against the saints. In order to seduce us to accept his counterfeit kingdom of an earthly global governance, he will promise a counterfeit salvation consisting of *security and prosperity* for all who will believe him and profess their allegiance to his utopian heaven on earth. Fear is the ultimate form by which he will accomplish his diabolical scheme.

Mankind will be seduced through fear that security and prosperity…shalom… cannot be achieved by any other means but to accede to the demands of and proclaim allegiance to the universal new global order.

Mankind will be seduced through fear that security and prosperity…shalom… cannot be achieved by any other means but to accede to the demands *of* and proclaim allegiance *to* the universal new global order seductively, yet surely, perpetrated upon the planet. People will panic in the growing spiritual vacuum that threatens to suck every man, woman and child into a false global faith. Hope will fail as horror sweeps the earth. Those not truly living by faith in the God of Truth will become spiritual casualties, willing to forfeit their souls for a mess of political pottage of false promises.

It is all happening now. The stage is set for *History's Final Act*. Satan will repose his power in a counterfeit savior reinforced by a false prophet who will purport to do miracles and wonders to convince the holdouts to succumb to the seduction. True saints will bear the brunt of the backlash of the brutal power that, through pursuit of proffered peace, will destroy many (Rev. 13:1-7, Dan. 8:25).

Satan's rage is ruthless. He intends to steal God's glory and government in and through Christ by shifting global worship to his counterfeit.

A shift in worship is the goal of this spiritual war being waged superficially (and therefore seductively) at the level of economics and politics. Satan's rage is ruthless. He intends to steal God's glory and government in and through Christ by shifting global worship to his counterfeit, the Anti-Christ. Virtually the whole earth will succumb to the seduction, shifting trust from the Prince of Peace (Jesus Christ) to the "son of perdition" (II Thess. 2:3, Rev. 13:2-8).

This shift of worship will be at great cost. It will cost anyone who purports to "worship" Satan's utopian global system and its leader his or her eternal destiny. It will forever deprive of access to *The Secret of the Lord* (Rev. 14:9-11). And the shift of "worship" and faith will be accomplished by fear.

FAITH IN THE FACE OF FEAR

It is crucial to remember and be convinced at this critical hour of history that "God hath not given us the spirit of fear: but of power, and of love, and of a sound mind" (II Tim. 1:7). God has promised that He will "keep him in perfect peace, whose mind is stayed on thee: because he trusteth in thee" (Isa. 26:3). Meditate on these passages of God's promise.

Trust in the Lord with ALL thine heart; and lean not unto thine own understanding. In ALL thy ways acknowledge him, and he shall direct thy path" (Prov. 2:5-6). "Be not wise in thine own eyes: fear the Lord, and depart from evil" (Prov. 3:7). Remember! *"The Secret of the Lord* is with them that fear him; and he will show them his covenant" (Psa. 25:14).

Prepare now for *History's Final Act*. Delay will pave the way for deception; and deception will define the broad way to eternal destruction, forever closing God's gate to discover *The Secret of the Lord*.

Time is growing short. Yeshua Messiah's Second Coming is near. Today...IF...you will hear His voice, harden not your heart. Repent! Prepare the *Way* of the Lord that leads to the *Secret* of the Lord.

Three times recently on my national radio broadcast, *VIEW-POINT*, Orthodox Jews from Jerusalem have openly declared their conviction of the soon appearance of the long awaited "Anointed One," the Messiah. They each separately stated, "We can hear the footsteps of the Messiah." Can you?

Today's choice will determine tomorrow's "chosen-ness" for ultimate and final access to *The Secret of the Lord*. Do not miss God's final call.

Chapter 17

PROVOCATIVE THOUGHTS FOR SECRET SEEKERS

1. Do you agree that mankind will soon stand in the ultimate "valley of decision"...either to fear God or to fear man? Why...or why not?

2. Why does discovering *The SECRET of the Lord* depend upon rediscovering the *fear of the Lord?*

3. What is Satan's coming counterfeit to *The SECRET of the Lord?*

4. How does fear of man neutralize faith in God?

5. In what ways is the stage being set for "History's Final Act?"

6. Is your fear of the Lord and trust in His promises such that you will not succumb to Satan's end-time seduction?

CHAPTER 18

Man's Final Mark

"The mercy of the Lord is from everlasting to everlasting upon them that fear Him..." (Psa. 103:17).

FINAL MEANS "FINAL." YET IT IS EXCEEDINGLY DIF-
ficult for us, living in a temporal world where business appears
to go on as usual from generation to generation, to conceive
of genuine finality concerning matters of life, except for death
itself. Life just seems to be one long continuum. This is particularly true for those privileged to live in relative prosperity.
For prosperity tends toward shift of trust from God to man,
whereas adversity tends to shift our ultimate trust back toward
our Creator as the final repose of hope, both in this life and in
the life to come.

THE BATTLE FOR TRUST

This uneasy balance reveals, in part, why man's trust in
God seems so tenuous. We are spiritual beings living in a physical world that continually tears us in our thoughts away from

our Creator, the lover of our souls. He longs to reveal His deepest secrets to us who are made in His image, yet we continually resist His proffered hope in search of happiness in the "secrets" of this age.

Our Creator...longs to reveal His deepest secrets to us...yet we continually resist His proffered hope in search of happiness in the "secrets" of this age.

Satan, the Deceiver, is well aware of this divided mind and heart in mankind, for he also dealt with it in the heavenlies, choosing rather to rebel and take its eternal risks than to reconcile himself as a created being to the eternal plans and purposes of his Creator. This "cosmic" battle for dominion over the mind of man has now reached the ultimate "moment of truth," and mankind now stands in history's final "valley of decision."

At stake in this historical battle is your trust. And trust is deeply rooted in your perception of truth. It is for that reason that the last two generations of world history have confronted mankind with an unprecedented assault on the very concept of "truth."

The entire philosophical base of this so-called "post-modern" age is that there is no absolute truth, that whatever "truth" there is cannot be known, and therefore your own thinking and experience are the sole and final arbiter of "truth" for you. God and His claim of absolute truth, with Jesus claim to be "the way, the truth and the life," are summarily dismissed as intellectually impossible concepts and therefore to be rejected.

Mankind's search for genuine meaning and hope has therefore become disconnected from the wisdom of the Creator, which alone could be absolutely trusted. We are left to drift, without divine direction, upon a disconcerting sea of relativity. And "hope deferred maketh the heart sick" (Prov. 13:12). The general condition of humankind on the near edge of Christ's Second Coming is heart sickness, with no hope or even meaningful diagnosis provided...that is, outside *The Secret of the Lord.*

God is not willing that this dismal and eternally-destructive condition continue in your life or in the life of any person. For God is "not willing that any should perish, but that all should come to repentance" (II Pet. 3:9). Satan, however, is dedicated to your eternal destruction. And he has a plan to ensure your destiny in eternal damnation, separation from God and being forever deprived of *The Secret of the Lord.* Your trust is the spoil of the battle.

SATAN'S FINAL METHOD

We have seen, in the previous chapter, the general outline of how the enemy of our souls seeks to take us captive to his camp through *History's Final Act.* We must now look meticulously at his method, which will explain the ultimate simplicity of God's Final Message.

Earthly fear is the antithesis of genuine faith. And genuine faith in God is rooted in belief *in* and commitment *to* the absolute truth of His Word, the Bible. Trust is the natural outflow of a growing love *of* and obedience *to* God's living Word. But if we are cut off from truth, trust languishes and we become captive to earthly fear. We are thus spiritually primed to shift our trust from God to man and his government and to replace any residual fear of the Lord with a growing and paralyzing fear of man. Enter...the "Mark of the Beast."

We are spiritually primed to shift our trust from God to man and his government and to replace fear of the Lord with a growing and paralyzing fear of man. Enter... the "Mark of the Beast."

Even the unbelieving world is not ignorant of the solemnity of our times. For a generation, the words "Apocalypse," "End of the World," "Armageddon" and "Mark of the Beast" have grown so common that even primary secular publications use these terms with increasing frequency. There is a growing sense, indeed expectation, that something of profound significance, unprecedented in history, is about to occur. And they are correct.

As the coming of a "New World Order" has been boldly and even brazenly announced beginning in 1991 by then President George H. W. Bush, its final fruition has now been declared by the first permanent president of the European Union in January 2010. He made clear that this long-awaited utopian plan for resurrecting the ancient Tower of Babel actually formally began at the G20 Summit in August of 2009. Take heed, therefore, because the infamous "mark" is being readied to recruit, by fear, the masses to worship a counterfeit "master."

The infamous "mark" is being readied to recruit, by fear, the masses to worship a counterfeit "master."

PROPHECY OF THE MARK

The *mark* is coming. God, in His great love and mercy, foretold through the prophet Daniel and through the apostle John that a great "beast" government would arise as man's final and ultimate expression of government without God. That final resurrected "Roman Empire" will be "exceedingly dreadful" (Dan. 7:19).

The power of this empire promising peace will be such as to deprive the citizens of the world of privacy in order to solidify its all-encompassing control. In order to accomplish such control, this beast "causeth all, both small and great, rich and poor, free and bond, to receive a mark in their right hand or in their foreheads" (Rev. 13:16). The Greek word translated "mark" means "scratch or etch." This mark signifies "the number of a man" which is "the number of the beast." That number is "Six hundred three-score and six" or 666 (Rev. 13:18).

There has been much speculation and theorization over the centuries, attempting to identify "the beast" by means of interpretation of the significance of the number 666. It is not our purpose here to engage in that particular discussion. The Scripture advises: "Let him that hath understanding count the number of the beast" (Rev. 13:18). It should be noted, however, that the number "7" signifies God and His perfection. The number "6" signifies man, "a little lower than the angels [or elohim]" (Psa. 8), but not equal to God. Man was given six days to do all his labor and the seventh he was to rest, showing his trust in God rather than in himself, or even in Creation (Gen. 2:3). The number "3" signifies God in His god-head, a word that occurs only three times in Scripture. It would appear then, at minimum, regardless of whatever else it may signify, that the number 666 is the number of man seeking godhood. Expressed in different terms, it is a man claiming to be as God heading up an earthly empire attempting, under Satan's authority, to replace God's authority in the earth in a final act of arrogant rebellion against a loving Creator.

PURPOSE OF THE MARK

The purpose of the "mark of the beast" is to confirm your identification with and your allegiance to mankind's ultimate expression of "SELF-government," without submission to man's Creator. Your willingness to carry that mark will reflect both the condition of your heart before God and your willingness to conform to the will and ways of a world system calculated to replace your trust in your Creator with trust in man.

The purpose of the mark…is of profound spiritual and eternal significance. It involves the necessity of making a choice.

The purpose of the mark, as you can well see, is of profound spiritual and eternal significance. It involves the necessity of making a choice. And that choice will be rendered more or less difficult by your true spiritual condition preceding the presentation of the mark. Jeremiah warned:

Cursed is the man that trusteth in man, and maketh flesh his arm, and whose heart departed from the Lord. But…Blessed is the man that trusteth in the Lord, and whose hope the Lord is (Jer. 17:5-7).

It is extremely important to note that the Scriptures give no indication that professing believers in Christ will not be faced with this profound choice. In fact, to the contrary, all of the warnings of Scripture are to believers. To conclude that "believers" are somehow exempt is to render the warnings of Christ, His apostles and the apostle Paul as meaningless.

The Scriptures give no indication that professing believers in Christ will not be faced with this profound choice. In fact… all of the warnings of Scripture are to believers.

Consider that Daniel, one of the three most righteous men in the Bible (Ezek. 14), faced a similar choice resulting in his being cast into the lion's den (Dan. 6). The three godly Hebrew young men who refused to bow down to Babylon's golden anti-God authority were cast into the fiery furnace (Dan. 3). And thousands of faithful first, second and third-century Christians met frightening fates in the Coliseum, refusing to recant their faiths by bowing down to Rome's rule that demanded they make a choice, either for Caesar or for Christ.

Once again the choice will be…Caesar or Christ. Rome ruled at Christ's first coming and will rule at His Second Coming. At Yeshua's first coming, the "evangelical" Pharisees and "mainline" Sadducees declared "We have no king but Caesar" (Jn. 19:15). What will you say

Once again the choice will be…Caesar or Christ.

by your life choices before Jesus' Second Coming? The presentation of the mark will profoundly test your trust. It will also seduce most men and women, through Satan's sleight-of-hand, to embrace the Deceiver's alternative "secret" to *the Secret of the Lord*, proffering "peace and prosperity" to the planet. It will be presented as the ultimate "salvation."

PRESENTATION OF THE MARK

The phenomenal advance of technology over the past half century is both historic and prophetic. Over the course of this writer's lifetime, the atomic bomb and neutron bomb, threatening global holocaust, now holds the world hostage. The unraveling of DNA is an unrivaled biological development, causing man to aspire now to compete with the Creator. The computer has rendered computation so quick, and the accumulation and processing of information so vast as to make available the life histories of every man, woman and child on earth, including their pictures, medical histories, biometric identification and financial affairs. Satellite systems now enable the tracking and positioning, within six feet, of every person on the globe. In the precise words of an international engineer for the Sony Corporation in conversation with this author…"The day is coming when we will be god."

That is the emerging spirit of the resurrecting Roman Empire, empowered by technology so astounding and seemingly unending as to cause a "little horn" to arise with "eyes like the eyes of man," speaking "great words against the Most High," standing up against Christ himself, the "Prince of princes," becoming the last "Caesar" to rule the earth (Dan. 7:8, 25; 8:25).

Jesus warned us just before His crucifixion to "Render unto Caesar the things which be Caesar's, and unto God the things which be God's" (Luke 20:25). But what happens when Caesar

What happens when Caesar claims Christ-hood and his roman-ized kingdom usurps the authority of the Kingdom of God?

claims Christ-hood and his romanized kingdom usurps the authority of the Kingdom of God? That is the picture portrayed in Scripture of one called the "son of perdition," the one in whom Satan invests final authority as the Deceiver, to draw all men to worship his counterfeit christ, thus making "Caesar" the savior of the world.

A Marked Man

A "marked man" is one who is identified in some way for a particular purpose, whether good or evil. Both your Creator and His arch, enemy, Satan, wants you to be a "marked man or woman."

When God would deliver Israel from their Egyptian "house of bondage" and from the iron furnace of Pharaoh, God, through Moses, instructed the children of Israel to mark their homes by painting the blood of the Passover lamb on their doorposts (Exod. 12). Pharaoh, a type of Satan and his antichrist, bellowed, "Who is the Lord, that I should obey his voice, to let Israel go" (Exod. 5:2)? Pharaoh had marked the people for slavery, but God marked those who would obey and trust Him for deliverance.

When Israel and then Judah refused to trust God as revealed by their rebellion and disobedience, God promised their destruction because He was "broken with their whorish heart," but as always, God said He would "yet leave a remnant" (Ezek. 5, 6:8-9). How would God identify the *remnant* to be spared? God instructed an angel with an ink-horn to "set a mark upon the foreheads of the men that sigh and that cry for all the abominations that be done...." To those not then bearing God's mark, other angels were instructed to go through the city, "and smite: let not your eye spare, neither have ye any pity." God instructed the angels to "begin at my sanctuary" (Ezek. 9:4-7).

It is critical to be "marked" by God! Men and women *marked* by God are those who, by faith, "paint" the "blood of the Lamb" on the "doorposts" of their life and heart, who come Out of Egypt and its spirit of bondage to Satan's ways, and who live in the humble holiness of obedience, being "a doer of the word, and not a hearer only, deceiving your own selves" (Jam. 1:22, Ezek. 33:7-33, Matt. 7:21-29, Heb. 12:14). It is also critical to note that though all Israel were "heirs according to the promise" and were the "seed of Abraham," most were not *marked* by God as the elect remnant because their life of purported faith did not reflect righteous living demanded by God of those who claimed to be His sons and daughters.

> *Satan…intends that you be a* marked *man or woman. He knows the unlikelihood that he can accomplish this directly, and so he relies upon seduction.*

Satan also intends that you be a *marked* man or woman. He knows the unlikelihood that he can accomplish this directly, and so he relies upon seduction. He is adept at employing simple deception to lead the unsuspecting to destruction. Ultimately, however, most will succumb and receive his mark. Lamentably, all "whose names are not written in the book of life of the Lamb…" will receive Lucifer's mark of worship of the end-time "Caesar" who will rule in his stead (Rev. 13:8, 14:9-10).

A Marketing Method

Mankind will not readily receive a mark that many or most find suspicious. Like all products and promises, it must be promoted. The people must be persuaded to forfeit principle for pragmatism, privacy for the promise of protection and provision marketed as *security* and *prosperity*. Even professing Christians must be targeted to compromise their trust.

The mark is being marketed by the gospel of gradualism. Technological advances are trumpeted as solutions for trying circumstances and troubling problems. Private convictions are gradually softened in favor of the purported public "common good." Headlines and commercials scream dire threats demanding technological salvation. Proliferating international drug trading, identity theft, economic meltdown and the terrifying prospect of terrorism conspire to induce compromise. Citizens demand solutions and politicians pander to provide security through governmental salvation. Trust is gradually, yet inexorably, shifted from God and His gospel to the government and global saviors. We have witnessed the willingness of American politicians, their president and the people they represent to abandon the very foundational principles of America's prosperity in order to purportedly "rescue" the world from financial collapse.

Dramatic technological developments in virtually every sphere of life, coupled with the explosion of the *Information Age*, have gradually normalized both the concept and practice of universal identification. Few give it much thought. Although fraught with corrupting consequences, most choose to embrace greater and more intrusive identification for the government-promised *security* and *prosperity*. Blood-bought freedom is cavalierly sacrificed on the altar of personal peace and prosperity.

All that remains... is an event of global significance, causing those increasingly addicted to security and prosperity to... forfeit freedom for a false faith in a God-defying global government to provide their needs.

The multitudinous rivulets of technological developments coursing down the mountains of commerce worldwide over the past fifty years have made their way to common expression in a global river sweeping everything in its path toward global government and global control, ostensibly for global security and prosperity or *shalom*.

Technology is marching lockstep to the incessant drumbeat of commercial globalism and global government. All that remains to complete "marketing" to the masses is an event of global significance, causing those increasingly addicted to *security* and *prosperity* to readily forfeit freedom for a false faith in a God-defying global government to provide their needs. The stage for the ultimate transactional exchange of trust in God to trust in man will have been set. That moment is accelerating at breathtaking speed. Has the most recent global economic meltdown precipitated such prophetic fulfillment? Are you ready? How about your family? And pastor, will your congregation stand the test?

PRESENTATION OF THE MARK

The technological groundwork for implementation of a global mark is nearing completion. Popular applications of supporting technologies are now readily received and resistence is diminishing. Demand for solutions to pervasive problems such as identity theft, counterfeiting, terrorism and drug trafficking is growing exponentially. And globalists wait patiently for the propitious moment and method to present their mark so that people will clamor for its promised benefits, willingly and with gratitude releasing precious freedoms for pernicious false promises of peace and prosperity.

The presentation of the mark will require a religious component to complete the deception. A miracle-working false prophet, called "another beast" will come up "out of the earth," exercising all the power of the first beast which the great whore rides (Rev. 13:11-13). This "beast" prophet will cause all who dwell on the earth, "both small and great, rich and poor, free and bond, to receive a mark in their right hand or in their foreheads" (Rev. 13:16). The purpose is to enforce and facilitate the power and control of the final beast government, the revived Holy Roman Empire, "that no man might buy or sell" without the mark, the name of the beast, or the number of his name" (Rev. 13:17).

This "beast" prophet will be very persuasive, capturing the minds and hearts of the vast majority into the seductive false trust of a counterfeit savior.

Spiritual deception will be accomplished "by means of those miracles" which the false prophet has "power to do in the sight of the beast." This "beast" prophet will be very persuasive, capturing the minds and hearts of the vast majority into the seductive false trust of a counterfeit savior. The apostle Paul reveals why people will be deceived (II Thess. 2:10-12):

1. "They love not the truth."
2. "They have pleasure in unrighteousness."

Protect yourself and those in your charge. Be a lover of God's truth. "Seek first the kingdom of God and His righteousness" (Matt. 6:33). "Trust in the Lord with all your heart; and lean not on your own understanding. In all your ways acknowledge Him, and He shall direct your paths" (Prov. 3:5-6).

THE POWER OF THE MARK

Possession of the *mark of the beast* on your person is a public declaration of your allegiance and submission to the power of the final "beast" empire...the resurrected Roman Empire. It is a testimony to your true trust.

The *mark of the beast* represents the promise and power of man to protect you and to provide for your needs. Since this final global empire is man's best and ultimate effort to govern without God and since the mark is the indicia of "a man" (Rev. 13:18) in whom Satan, the master deceiver, will "incarnate" himself as a false christ, a person's choice to receive that mark, regardless of whatever rationalization he may conjure up, will have the power to separate or "sanctify" that person unto Satan, thus eternally depriving him/her of *The Secret of the Lord*.

The mark becomes powerful leverage to compel every man, woman and child to bow to the beast. The only powers over which the beast and its mark have no ultimate dominion are the power of God and your power to choose. Satan, through his anti-christ, will be very persuasive, however. His persuasive power, as the "son of perdition," is the power of life or death. Your choice will be perceived as a choice of life or death on earth. If you do not receive the mark, you will be unable to buy or sell within the global economic system, thus jeopardizing survival. You may also risk execution as a traitor to the Empire, just as it was for the early Christians.

If you receive the mark in fear rather than reject it by faith, you will have failed the ultimate and final test of your trust.

On the other hand, if you receive the mark in fear rather than reject it by faith, you will have failed the ultimate and final test of your trust. Those who take the mark will do so, from God's perspective, as an act of worship of deified man and of the Deceiver, Satan. Therefore, taking of the mark also has the power to deprive you of eternal life with our Lord Jesus Christ, the God of Creation, and His "secret."

Choosing to receive the mark promises temporal peace, provision and security. Choosing to reject the *mark of the beast* may result in loss of earthly life but in the gaining of eternal peace and salvation. "If any man worship the beast and his image, and receive his mark in his forehead, or in his hand, the same shall drink of the wine of the wrath of God...and he shall be tormented with fire and brimstone in the presence of the holy angels, and in the presence of the Lamb" (Rev. 14:9-10).

PERMANENCY OF THE MARK

The historic battle between God and Satan is a battle for your soul. The *mark of the beast* is not just some clever marketing device but will determine your eternal destiny.

To receive the *mark of the beast* is to reveal your true heart. It reveals what you truly value—the temporal or the eternal. Isaac had two sons, Jacob and Esau. Esau foolishly sold his precious birthright, as the first-born, for a mess of pottage (Gen. 28:7-9). God despised Esau for treating trivially that which had true value. Therefore said the Lord, "Jacob have I loved, but Esau have I hated" (Rom. 9:13, Mal. 1:3).

Where do you place your true value? What would those around you say? Where do you invest your time, your talent, your treasure? Do you seek first the kingdom of God and His righteousness? If that does not define your life now, how will it suddenly become foremost when your very life is on the line?

No one can definitively and precisely say how or when the *mark of the beast* will ultimately be presented or what form it will have. There are many theories. Some say it will be a computer chip. Others say it will be some mark of the first-day Sabbath as ordered by the *Pontifex Maximus* of ancient Rome and re-confirmed by the Papacy contrary to the fourth commandment. Yet others have said it will be the six-pointed star or the mere number 666. The Scriptures merely call it a mark or "etching." The important thing is to recognize and understand what that mark represents, that from God's viewpoint it is a declaration of where you choose to put your trust, and that once made, the choice is permanent.

A national news article titled, "The Dangerous Art of the Tattoo," observed that "Tattoos are fast becoming a mark of the 21st century." At least 25% of people under 30 in America now sport at least one tattoo. Marks and piercings of the body have become normalized on the near edge of Christ's Second Coming as never before in history. Dr. Bernadine Healy notes, "…most people get tattooed without a clue about the implications." The risks, she warns, are significant, "the most obvious one being a major case of remorse." Unfortunately, notes Dr. Healy, "tattooing is designed to last forever."

The *mark of the beast*, whatever it may actually prove to be and whatever form it may take, will be permanent. It will reflect a permanent and unchangeable choice. The mark demonstrates a choice of faith, trust and worship, regardless of whatever rationalizing "spin" one might employ to justify receiving it. God's warnings are direct, they are dire, and they determine eternal destiny.

Anyone who chooses to receive the mark of identification indicating trust in the counterfeit christ, his false miracle-working prophet, and his Creator-defying and denying system of salvation, will not have their names "written in the book of life of the Lamb slain from the foundation of the world" (Rev. 13:8). Consider well!

All that dwell upon the earth shall worship him [the counterfeit christ representing the final beast empire] whose names are not written in the book of life of the Lamb..." (Rev. 13:8).

By far, the majority, both Jew and Gentile, will display their trust in a false christ representing Satan's kingdom. Yeshua specifically warned his Jewish brethren, "I am come in my Father's name, and ye receive me not: if another shall come in his own name [the counterfeit christ or self-anointed one], him ye will receive" (Jn. 5:43).

"If any man worship the beast and his image, and receive his mark in his forehead, or in his hand, the same shall drink the wine of the wrath of God...." "And they have no rest day or night, who worship the beast and his image, and whoever receiveth the mark of his name" (Rev. 14:9-11). "...there fell a noisome and grievous sore upon the men which had the mark of the beast, and upon them which worshiped his image" (Rev. 16:1-2).

PEOPLE "NOT APPOINTED TO WRATH"

Many have devised theological systems to purportedly prevent professing believers in Yeshua from being faced with and having to make the profound choice discussed in this chapter. Such systems may themselves be dangerously deceptive, for if we do not believe we may face such a challenge to our faith and trust, it induces weakness, spiritual indolence, and great susceptibility to the seduction that will lure most to receive the mark. Remember, all of the end-time warnings of Scripture are to professing believers. Therefore, the wise believer will prepare for the worst and hope for the best, always cementing our confidence in Christ.

If we do not believe we may face such a challenge to our faith and trust, it induces weakness, spiritual indolence, and great susceptibility to the seduction that will lure most to receive the mark.

"Yourselves know perfectly that the day of the Lord so cometh as a thief in the night." "But ye, brethren, are not in darkness, that that day should overtake you as a thief." "Therefore, let us not sleep, as do others; but let us watch and be sober [serious minded]." "Let us, who are of the day, be sober, putting on the breastplate of faith and love; and for an helmet, the hope of salvation. For God hath not appointed us to wrath…" (I Thess. 5:2-9).

The Bible references three main sources of wrath: the wrath of Satan, the wrath of man and the wrath of God. The "wrath of God" is reserved for the unbeliever (Jn. 3:36) and will also be poured out on "the children of disobedience." The apostle Paul warns believers, "Let no man deceive you with vain words: for because of these things [unrighteous living] cometh the wrath of God upon the children of disobedience" (Eph. 5:1-11).

The wrath of God is reserved for those who reject Yeshua as His Anointed One, who refuse to trust Jesus Christ as Savior, who reveal their lack of love and trust by rebellion and disobedience and who shift their ultimate trust and allegiance in time of testing to Satan's counterfeit kingdom and false christ. "Here is the patience of the saints," however. Saints that are not seduced "are they that keep the commandments of God, and the faith of Jesus" (Rev. 14:12).

Praise God that He has not appointed those who truly love and trust Jesus Christ, as evidenced by their faithful lives, to the outpouring of His wrath. God has and will prepare a way of escape from the final and unprecedented outpouring of His wrath. God's fury of righteous indignation brought as judgment on the earth is not to be trifled with. The remnant who are truly faithful will be "raptured" or "caught up" to meet the Lord (I Thess. 4:16-17), just as His wrath is ready to be out-poured, beginning at the Sixth Seal,

The wrath of God is reserved for those... who refuse to trust Jesus Christ as Savior, who reveal their lack of love and trust by rebellion and disobedience and who shift their ultimate trust and allegiance in time of testing to Satan's counterfeit kingdom and false christ.

"for the great day of [God's] wrath is come; and who shall be able to stand" (Rev. 6:17)? Little wonder that Paul enjoined, "… comfort one another with these words" (I Thess. 4:18).

While true believers are protected from the wrath of God, the Scripture provides no assurance that believers will be protected from the end-time wrath of man. On the contrary, Jesus and the apostles repeatedly warned of the last days assault against Christ and his true followers. "Then shall they deliver you up to be afflicted, and shall kill you: and ye shall be hated of all nations for my name's sake." Notice, it is not the name of **God** that will be deemed offensive but the name of **Jesus**. "Then shall many be offended, and shall betray one another…." This betrayal will most likely

Notice, it is not the name of God that will be deemed offensive but the name of Jesus.

be by those who fail the trust test by receiving the mark, betraying true believers to deliver them over to the Roman system that

Jesus warned, "...he that shall endure to the end, the same shall be saved."

persecuted believers in the early church and will multiply that persecution against the end-time church, in great fury. For this reason, Jesus warned, "But he that shall endure to the end, the same shall be saved" (Matt. 24:9-13).

PREPARE YOUR LIFE

The pictures portrayed by the end-time prophecies of both Old and New Covenants are, to the natural man, terrifying. Jesus warned of "Men's hearts failing them for fear, and for looking after those things which are coming upon the earth..." (Luke 21:26). Daniel warned that the "little horn" anti-christ power "made war with the saints, and prevailed against them" (Dan. 7:21). The counterfeit christ, given over totally to Satan, will blatantly blaspheme against God, "and it was given over unto him to make war with the saints, and to overcome them..." (Rev. 13:7).

How then should we live? How will you stand in the evil day? Will you walk in fear...or in faith? Will you live in trust... or in terror? Today is the day to decide, before the final deception makes it a hundred times more difficult.

"Finally, my brethren, be strong in the Lord, and in the power of his might. Put on the whole armor of God, that ye may be able to stand against the wiles of the devil." "Stand therefore, having your loins girt about with truth, and having on the breastplate of righteousness." "Above all, taking the shield of faith, wherewith ye shall be able to quench all the fiery darts of the wicked. And take the helmet of salvation, and the sword of the Spirit, which is the Word of God." "Praying always...and watching...with all perseverance" (Eph. 6:10-18).

"The great dragon was cast out, that old serpent, called the Devil and Satan, which deceiveth the whole world: he was cast into the earth, and his angels were cast out with him" (Rev. 12:9).

They accused the brethren continuously. And how do we overcome him? Here are the three most important things to remember for spiritual victory. Process these prayerfully. "And they overcame him (1) by the blood of the Lamb, and (2) by the word of their testimony [their life matches their profession of faith]; and (3) they loved not their lives unto death" (Rev. 12:11). Be warned, "for the devil is come down unto you with great wrath, because he knoweth that he hath but a short time" (Rev. 12:12).

PROTECTED BY GOD'S MARK

Satan has his mark, but God also has His mark. One is a mark of eternal destruction, the other a mark of eternal deliverance. "The foundation of God standeth sure, having this seal, The Lord knoweth them that are his. And let everyone that nameth the name of Christ depart from iniquity" (II Tim. 2:19). If we name the name of Christ, the only name by which we can be saved, God expects us to depart from the sinful ways that define those who will ultimately take the Deceiver's mark.

Satan has his mark, but God also has His mark. One is a mark of eternal destruction, the other a mark of eternal deliverance.

Immediately before God pours out His wrath, he instructs an angel "having the seal of the living God" to seal "the servants of our God in their forehead." Which seal will you receive…the seal of God… or the mark of the beast? Will your trust be in man…or the MASTER? God's loving "Clue" revealing history's conclusion is found in His final message to man.

Chapter 18

PROVOCATIVE THOUGHTS FOR SECRET SEEKERS

1. What is the real purpose of *the mark of the beast?*

2. In what ways does receiving that mark reveal where a person truly puts his or her trust?

3. How do you think the *mark* of the beast empire will be marketed so that the vast majority, even professing believers, will accept it?

4. What are the two clear spiritual reasons the Apostle Paul gave as to why professing believers will be deceived?

5. What part will *fear of man* vs. *fear of God* play in choosing the mark of the beast?

6. Caesar…or Christ? Which will you choose in which to place your trust? Are you prepared for this test?

7. What steps can you take to prepare your life and the lives of those in your spheres of influence to pass this ultimate test of trust?

CHAPTER 19

God's Final Message

"Then...all the remnant of the people, obeyed the voice of the Lord their God...and the people did fear before the Lord" (Hag. 1:12).

HISTORY'S FINAL MOMENT IS RAPIDLY APPROACHING. It is for such a time as this that God, the Creator of all things, has reserved delivery of His *Final Message* to mankind. His great concern is that we will be seduced to follow a surrogate rather than His "secret." And He well knows the consequences will be horrifyingly devastating. His mercy and kindness, therefore, mandate this divine moment of decision. It is proclaimed in a simple message distilling, for destiny, the good news of His "secret."

THE BEAST...THE BLESSING

A great "beast" power has arisen in the earth and is preparing to declare dominion. "All the world wondered after the beast," and "they worshiped the beast..." (Rev. 13:1-3). The beast has a religious spokesman, a false prophet. This false prophet "deceiveth them that dwell on the earth" by means of "great wonders and miracles" (Rev. 13:13-14). And by means of his seductive deception,

> He causeth all, both small and great, rich and poor, free and bond, to receive a mark in their right hand, or in their foreheads: and that no man might buy or sell, save he that had the mark, or the name of the beast, or the number of his name" (Rev. 13:16-17).

This "mark of the beast" will be promoted as promising the ultimate earthly blessing of "security and prosperity," "peace and prosperity"…"shalom." Yet its temporary promise will rapidly deteriorate into devastating pain. Loss of freedom will cause faith to languish and fear to proliferate. Promised blessing will become an agonizingly baneful cry. Hope will dissolve in progressive horror, causing men and women to curse God rather than the Deceiver.

This "mark of the beast" will be promoted as promising the ultimate earthly blessing of "security and prosperity," "peace and prosperity"… "shalom."

Yet, for now, God's beneficent hand is reached out still. He is not willing that any should perish, but that all should come to repentance, embracing His love and costly salvation with humility of heart. Unfortunately, the Creator's promised blessing to those who truly believe in, trust, and obey Him seems to those demanding instant gratification to be unduly demanding and illusory. Thus, the "secret" of the Lord eludes their grasp even as panic leads them to perdition.

THE ANGELIC MESSAGE

The Lord of Creation desires to be the Lord of your life. Despite our stubbornness, rebellion and waywardness, His hand of hope is reached out still, yearning that we will hear and obey His voice calling us to reconciliation and righteousness through repentance. Yet the prophesied "Day of the Lord" is coming. It is now "at the door." And the God of love, who is also the God of truth, justice and judgment, is preparing to make a final call to His creation to "Prepare the Way of the Lord" in their lives. The *Revelation* of Jesus Christ, the final book of the Bible, portrays precisely how that final judicial notice of heavenly "due process" will be given. That final message to man immediately follows warning of the soon-coming "Mark of the Beast" and precedes God's warning of divine wrath to be poured out upon those who receive that notorious mark.

The final message from God to man is to be delivered by an angel to all who dwell on the earth.

The final message from God to man is to be delivered by an angel to all who dwell on the earth.

And I saw another angel fly in the midst of heaven, having the everlasting gospel to preach unto them that dwell on the earth, and to every nation, and kindred, and tongue, and people (Rev. 14:6).

Notice carefully! This is God's *final message* proclaiming the *gospel* (good news) to mankind. It is designed and delivered to be both heard and heeded. It will not be missed. In point of fact, even as you now read it, you will, in effect, have "heard" it and be beholden to heed it. The message is profoundly simple, yet simply profound. Here it is for your consideration. It offers final hope of access to *The Secret of the Lord.*

Fear God, and give glory to Him: for the hour of His judgment is come: and worship Him who made heaven, and earth…" (Rev. 14:7).

This is the distilled gospel message of the entire Scripture. The message has three distinct parts, each of which complements the other in a "trinity" of truth. We must first look at each separately and then combine them in order to appreciate their collective significance. These are the three essential elements setting the final heavenly stage for eternal salvation and access to *The Secret of the Lord.*

NUMBER 1: FEAR GOD!
NUMBER 2: GIVE GLORY TO GOD AS GOD.
NUMBER 3: WORSHIP GOD AS CREATOR.

WHAT DOES IT MEAN TO "FEAR GOD?"

It should be obvious by now that what the Scriptures refer to as *the fear of the Lord* is of profound import from God's viewpoint. God, as our Creator, desires that we, as His creation, share His outlook, perspective and viewpoint, on the issues of life and eternity. When we refuse to do so, we, in effect, elevate ourselves and our own thinking to be equal to God. Such an attitude, from God's viewpoint, is pure rebellion against His authority, rulership and kingdom. To put it bluntly, it is treasonous against God and his rulership in "the kingdom of God." It prevents us from entering His kingdom and from sharing in its benefits. It forecloses access to *The Secret of the Lord.*

To FEAR GOD is first to recognize that He is GOD and GOD alone...that there is no other true God.

To *FEAR GOD* is first to recognize that He is GOD and GOD alone...that there is no other true God. Having recognized in both mind and heart that He is truly GOD, we are brought to an awesome respect of His position, His power, His person and His purposes. Such awesome and unmatched respect reduces us to awesome humility before Him who has power over heaven and earth. We would not dare to trifle with His truth. We would not

entertain waffling upon His will. We would not consider purporting to disagree with His Word. And we would quiver at the
mere prospect of deviating from His ways.

To the extent you or I cannot relate to a holy and righteous
God expecting such honor, reflected in an expectation of our
persistent and humble obedience, we must seriously question
whether we, in fact, know the God of the Bible. The Scriptures
make clear of Jesus Christ, that "by Him were all things created,
that are in heaven and earth" (Col. 1:13-17, Heb. 1:1-3), and that
He is "the same yesterday, today and forever" (Heb. 13:8).

The *fear of the Lord* includes not only a sense of awesome
respect and honor, but also a gravity of mind and heart that
would not dare to differ from his government for apprehension of incurring His holy wrath, which will be poured out
upon "the children of disobedience" (Col. 3:6).

The Apostle Paul makes special mention that to disregard
the wrath of God is to be "deceived with vain words" (Eph.
5:6). Indeed, "The fear of the Lord is the beginning of wisdom"
(Psa. 111:10). Without the genuine *fear of the Lord* we will neither welcome His salvation nor walk in *The Secret of the Lord.*

"Fear God," declares the urgent, final angelic warning. Do
you truly fear God?

GIVE GLORY TO GOD AS GOD

It is one thing to believe IN God, but it is quite another
thing to BELIEVE God. It is one thing to believe that God exists,
yet quite another to trust and obey Him
AS God. Mankind's persistent problem
with the Potentate of our souls, the God
of Creation, has not been so much our
unwillingness to recognize rhetorically
His existence but to resolve to reconcile
to His authority, thus giving Him glory.

It is one thing to believe IN God...yet quite another to trust and obey Him AS God.

As human beings created in God's image, we are incessantly tempted to either compete with or seek to usurp God's glory. This was the gravamen of Satan's iniquity. He craved to be like the Most High God. He lusted after God's glory. He refused to joyfully acquiesce in the role and relationship God had designed for him to fill, thus destroying fellowship and defining an eternal destiny separated from God. Ever since Satan's banishment from the realms of glory, he has been intent upon drawing mankind into the same defilement of God's glory. We therefore face a continued battle of mind and heart. Will we, or will we not, glorify God by exalting His Word, His will and His ways over our own designs and distorted viewpoints.

At no time in history has this battle for the glorification of man over the glorification of God been more vehemently and boldly waged. It is a no-holds-barred warfare that will determine eternal destiny.

This gradual tarnishing of the glory of God in heart, thought and action progressively closes the gate to The Secret of the Lord, *until, at last, it is latched and locked.*

To give God glory is to "add weight to" His person, position and power in the estimation of people on earth and before the heavenly host. We give God glory by our prayers and praises. We exalt Him before men by openly agreeing with Him, conforming our words, wills, and ways to that which pleases God as expressed in the entirety of the Scriptures. We defile, defame and deface His glory by disagreeing with His Word, by behaving contrary to His ways and by shifting our allegiance and trust from God to man.

This shifting of trust from the Master to man and from God to earthly government occurs progressively. Few intend to blatantly abandon their trust in God or to tarnish His glory. Yet we do. We allow our fleshly or carnal nature to drive an increasingly hard bargain with our faith. Give the flesh an inch and it will lay claim to your soul and begin to rub the gloss from God's glory. Before long, God's glory has all but vanished in the victory of the flesh, so that SELF or man might be glorified. This gradual tarnishing of the glory of God in heart, thought and action progressively closes the gate to *The Secret of the Lord*, until, at last, it is latched and locked.

God's glory is of great moment as history's final hour rapidly approaches. As mankind yields to the global spirit to shift trust from God to a global government, and to continually "diss" what God has called humanity to obey, we are then in grave danger of losing the glory of God in our lives, our families, our nations…indeed in the entire earth. This is Satan's end-time goal…to globally co-opt the glory of God.

Israel well understands, at least historically, the gravity of losing and defaming the glory of God. Through rebellion and dis-obedience of people and priest alike, the high priest's grandson was named "Ichabod," meaning "the glory has departed…" (I Sam. 4:21). When the glory is departed, God's grace becomes in short supply, until His glory is restored. Our times will not allow us the luxury of testing this truth.

When the "son of perdition" is revealed and begins to breathe blasphemy against God and His Messiah…the stakes for glorifying God will become grave beyond measure.

The history of man is waiting to be written. Your name will either be written "in the earth" (Jn. 17:13) or in God's "Book of Life" (Rev. 13:8). We must all choose. If you make the choice, God (by His grace or enabling power) will help you make the necessary changes to glorify Him. But choose now!

When the "son of perdition" is revealed and begins to breathe blasphemy against God and His Messiah throughout the earth, the stakes for glorifying God will become grave beyond measure. This Satanic "incarnation" known as the Anti-christ "opposeth and exalteth himself above all that is called God, or that is worshiped; so that he as God sitteth in the temple of God, shewing himself that he is God" (II Thess. 2:4).

Given the dire and dramatic nature of this final assault on God's glory, it should be warmly gratifying to those who love God and who are called according to His purpose through Yeshua, the Messiah, that God has seen fit to forewarn mankind:

Fear God, and give glory to him (Rev. 14:7).

God, in His mercy, then tells us truthfully the reason why this simple instruction is of ultimate import for mankind. Simply stated…

For the hour of His judgment is come (Rev. 14:7).

WHY WORSHIP GOD AS CREATOR?

"Worship Him that made heaven and earth…" is the third mandate of the angelic message to mankind (Rev. 14:7). But why must such a mandate be so explicitly stated? And why reiterate that which would otherwise seem so obvious throughout human history? It is precisely because of the profound positioning of our times in the "last days" of prophetic time that renders the mandate of intense significance. Simply stated, *The Secret of the Lord* is cut off from those who do not recognize and give worship to God as Creator.

The Secret of the Lord *is cut off from those who do not recognize and give worship to God as Creator.*

The Bible begins with the words, "In the beginning God created…" (Gen. 1:1). We are then clearly told that "…God created heaven and earth" (Gen. 1:1). The balance of the first chapter of Scripture, the Word of God, then tells the reader that God created ALL things, both animate and inanimate, on the earth and in the cosmos. He is making the most important declaration of history, both of earth and of the universe. He is declaring that He IS God, and that this is the beginning of human understanding and wisdom.

After establishing that fact of faith, He declares, with dramatic comparison to the rest of creation, that "God created man in His own image, in the image of God created He him, male and female created he them" (Gen. 1:26-27). Without these facts of faith, human existence has no ultimate meaning and the Bible has no legitimate authority. In reality, *The Secret of the Lord* rises or falls with both accepting and declaring that God is Creator of all things and worshiping Him as that Creator, who is worthy of our praise and glory.

> **The Secret of the Lord** *rises or falls with both accepting and declaring that God is Creator of all things and worshiping Him as that Creator.*

This has been the nearly universal understanding of mankind throughout recorded history, regardless of religious persuasion. Few have been so bold as to deny either the existence of *God* or of the necessity that some power other and greater than ourselves brought the worlds into existence. For this reason, the psalmist wrote, "The fool hath said in his heart, There is no God" (Ps. 14:1, 53:1).

The apostle Paul, speaking of the times in which we live, wrote, "That which may be known of God is manifest [obvious]…" (Rom. 1:19). Continuing to address this heart issue, he warned,

> *For the invisible things of Him from the creation of the world are clearly seen, being understood by the things that are made, even His eternal power and Godhead; so that they are without excuse (Rom. 1:20).*

This great Jewish apostle then exposed the heart issue at hand and its consequence, culminating in God's judgment. Read carefully his concern.

When they knew God, they glorified Him not AS GOD, neither were thankful [willing to render appropriate worship and praise]; but became vain in their imaginations, and their foolish heart was darkened.

Professing themselves wise, they became fools...Who changed the truth of God into a lie, and worshiped and served the creature more than the Creator....

As they did not like to retain God in their knowledge, God gave them over to a reprobate mind...(Rom. 1:21-28).

The consequences of denying God as Creator, essentially *deifying* man and nature, are profoundly troubling and perverse as to our lives on earth but are terrifying when contemplating eternal destiny and relationship (or lack thereof) to a holy God (Rom. 1:28-32). The risks of defiantly rejecting or doubting God as Creator are incalculable, including eternal forfeiture of *The Secret of the Lord*. Is this a risk-reward balance you are willing to resolve in favor of evolution and natural selection? In reality, you will either believe God, or men pretending to speak as "god," who baptize their god-less "faith" in the rubric of science.

> *The consequences of denying God as Creator...are terrifying when contemplating eternal destiny and relationship to a...holy God...including eternal forfeiture of* The Secret of the Lord.

We must then explore these alternative "faiths," because many have been unsuspectedly seduced by an anti-christ spirit being marketed to mankind by the deceptive dogma of a monstrous deception masquerading as science. We will now look in greater detail at the nature and extent of man's final assault against God's final message. Will fraudulent "science" foreclose your discovery of *The Secret of the Lord*? This is not a matter for idle banter or for intellectual argument, because eternal destiny rides in the balance. Please read the following chapter prayerfully, with an open heart.

Chapter 19

PROVOCATIVE THOUGHTS FOR
SECRET SEEKERS

1. How can the desire and demand for "instant grati-fication" seduce a person to abandon pursuit of *The SECRET of the Lord* and accept a false substitute?

2. What is God's "final message" to man?

3. What does it mean to "fear God?"

4. How can we "give glory to God as God?"

5. Why is acknowledging God as "Creator" so critical to discovering *The SECRET of the Lord?*

CHAPTER 20

"Science" vs. The Secret

"[they] changed the truth of God into a lie, and worshiped and served the creature more than the Creator…" (Rom.1:25).

SCIENCE CAN BE DECEPTIVE. IN FACT, SCIENCE CAN be and is seductively deceptive precisely because of how people popularly perceive it. Also, contrary to popular notions, science has profound spiritual implications and applications. And men, wielding "science" as a spiritual weapon, are intent on destroying your soul and depriving you of *The Secret of the Lord* through deception.

"PURE" SCIENCE IS NOT PURE

To use the term "pure science" is a virtual oxymoron. The reason is that every scientist, wittingly or unwittingly, brings to his or her "scientific" endeavor a host of isms and viewpoints that can, either overtly or covertly, affect the choice of projects promoted, the plan of inquiry, the perception for interpreting

195

data, and even pre-conceived conclusions. The public is not usually privy to these hidden and undisclosed pre-conceptions and false-real conclusions. Hence, "pure science" is not truly *pure*.

The pretense of scientific purity, however, is what prevails in the public mind. It is the *pretense* of purity that seduces the unsuspecting to sacrifice true principles, practices and profound beliefs on the altar of science.

SCIENT-ISM MAY NOT BE SURE

Scientism is the collection of attitudes and practices considered typical of scientists. It is based on the belief that the investigative methods of the physical sciences are applicable to all fields of inquiry, including the spiritual. The *scientific method* is the systematic procedure for scientific investigation involving observation of phenomena, experimentation to test the hypothesis, and a conclusion that validates, modifies, or rejects the hypothesis.

Scientists, using the scientific method, have brought and continue to bring amazing advances to modern life in nearly every field of genuine scientific exploration. Yet science has its limits. It can be used for good or for destruction. It can serve us or enslave us.

Science...has come to be seen in the modern and post-modern mind not just as a means of finding truth but rather as the mediator of truth.

Science itself has become a modern "ism." It has come to be seen in the modern and post-modern mind not just as a means of finding truth but rather as the *mediator* of truth. Rather than being our servant, it has become our master. The Spirit of the Creator which once governed and enervated the mind to legitimate and humble inquiry has been supplanted by the spirit of science which, in pride and illegitimate pursuit of power, seeks to silence the voice and remaining vestiges of the Creator.

A False Gospel

Science itself becomes a false gospel. It presents itself as a false gospel when it presents its theories as *gospel truth*. When a theory is presented and marketed to the public as an idea or concept to be accepted without question and without proof, science has breached the wall of its own self-limitations, taking on the extra-scientific aura of philosophy and religious belief. Science has thus, since the middle of the nineteenth century, *evolved* into a new ism…a virtual *religious* belief system with its own dogma and high priests.

> *Science has…evolved into a new ism…a virtual* religious *belief system with its own dogma and high priests.*

A Serious Dilemma

The ultimate issue subject to scientific exploration and hypothesis is the origin of all things, more particularly the origin of living things. The crown of this scientific conundrum is the origin of man. The potential answer to the question of the origin of things material, life, and ultimately humankind poses a profound problem for the world of science, and indeed, for the entire world.

The explanation of origins presents a serious dilemma of monumental proportions, indeed eternal proportions, for it thrusts the theories of science into a no-holds-barred, battle-to-the-death confrontation with the biblical proclamation of truth as to the origin of all things, including man. You and I, indeed

> *The explanation of origins presents a serious dilemma of…eternal proportions, for it thrusts the theories of science into a no-holds-barred, battle-to-the-death…with the biblical proclamation of truth as to the origin of all things, including man.*

the inhabitants of the entire planet, are caught in the cross-fire of this war. Most have taken sides. Ultimately, it is a battle for the mind and heart of every man, woman and child. As with many (perhaps most) wars, its' true underlying motivations are camouflaged by the now-sacred robes of science.

Lurking within the question of origins are fundamental questions over which the battle lines are drawn.

- Was mankind created, or did he evolve naturally?
- Does mankind have a greater purpose than do animals?
- Is mankind accountable for his attitudes and actions? If so, to whom or what?
- Does mankind have any hope beyond the grave?

A CONFLUENCE OF ISMS

Historically, scientists, while pursuing answers and explanations in the natural world, did their investigative work with an over-arching consciousness that the secrets of this amazingly ordered world could only be truly uncovered because there was an originating intelligence that designed it. A distinct element of humility and increasing awe graced the scientist's exploration. But gradually, as the nineteenth century progressed, the "spirit" of science and scientific endeavor began to change. A search was on to explain the origin of things, in particular man, outside of the revelation of Biblical Scripture. That change was merging with emerging new isms in other fields of thought.

A new, virulent humanism exploded upon the world stage through the French Revolution; erecting the "Goddess of Reason" while purporting to topple the God of the Bible and all legitimate authority of faith and family.

A new, virulent *humanism* exploded upon the world stage through the French Revolution; erecting the "Goddess of

198

Reason" while purporting to topple the God of the Bible and all legitimate authority of faith and family.

Into this vacuum of authority came new political, social and religious isms. George Friedrich Hegel, abandoning traditional concepts of biblical spirituality, sought to explain the material world through newly conceived "spiritual" principles, a "dialectic" or method of reasoning of: Thesis, antithesis and synthesis. He envisioned a political utopia that could be synthesized by a kind of political evolution called Hegelianism. Karl Marx merged the method of Hegel with a message of *scientific socialism*, luring one-third of the world's people into a man-centered, God-defying *communism*.

It should not come as an historical surprise, then, that into this hot bed of radical new isms should come the modern and post-modern world's "synthesis" of origins, called *Darwinism*.

Charles Darwin introduced his *Origin of Species* in 1859, in which he proposed his theory of natural selection. "He knew full well what he was up to," notes *NEWSWEEK*. "As early as 1844, he famously wrote to a friend that to publish his thoughts on evolution would be akin to 'confessing a murder'." "To a society accustomed to searching for truth in the pages of the Bible, Darwin introduced the notion of evolution… rather than as Genesis would have it."[1]

If God does not exist or did not create, who has authority in our lives and in our world?

By 1871, Darwin released his *Descent of Man*, claiming that man and ape could have developed from the same ancestor. The shock waves swept the world, eventually reforming the viewpoint of pastors, presidents, popes and most people as to the origin of all things, including man. It was not by the hand…or voice…of God, but by natural selection. "To a world taught to see the hand of God in every part of Nature, he suggested a different creative force altogether, an undirected, morally-neutral process he called natural selection."[2]

If God did not create as stated in Genesis 1, does God exist? If Genesis 1-11 is not true, can any of the rest of the Bible be believed? Does Scripture carry any moral or spiritual authority? If Scripture does not have ultimate authority and if God does not exist or did not create, who has authority in our lives and in our world?

Dr. Douglas Patina, author of an anti-creationist book, as quoted by Henry Morris, writes, "Creation and evolution between them exhaust the possible explanations for the origin of living things. Organisms either appeared on earth fully developed or they did not. If they did not, they must have developed from pre-existing species…. If they did appear in a fully developed state, they must indeed have been created by some omnipotent intelligence."[3] It is CREATION vs. NATURALISM. This is where science and biblical faith collide. Ultimately, it is not science at stake, but your soul. The real question remains…"Hath God said…?" Scientists well know the consequences. Do you?

CREATION vs. NATURALISM… is where science and biblical faith collide. Ultimately, it is not science at stake, but your soul.

NATURALISM VS. CREATION

Here is a clear-cut choice. The culture would seek to overlay the simplicity of this choice with a blanket of alleged complexity, spewing pseudo science to create a fog of obfuscation and confusion. In a world where the majority are convinced that "science does not lie" and that scientists have no ulterior motives for their projects and papers, naturalism wrapped in the concealing robe of "science" is both seductive and deceptive. The consequences of your choice are vast, beyond imagination. *VIEWPOINT DETERMINES DESTINY!*

Naturalism is a belief system. Just as it requires an element of faith to believe in CREATION, so it requires faith to believe in natural selection. In fact, it requires massive faith…irrational faith…to believe that nature, the physical world, has created itself from nothing.

Naturalism defies the most basic, accepted laws of science. The Second Law of Thermodynamics, called the Law of Entropy, declares that all matter and energy, all of the physical world, is in the process of steady deterioration and that such deterioration is inevitable and cannot be avoided, just as the Bible declares. Sir Isaac Newton gave us the accepted and unrefuted "Laws of Motion." They include:

It requires massive faith…irrational faith…to believe that nature, the physical world, has created itself from nothing. Naturalism defies the most basic, accepted laws of science.

1. A body at rest tends to remain at rest until acted upon by some outside force.
2. A body in motion tends to remain in motion until acted upon by some outside force.

Using simple logic as a reasonable person, it should be obvious that if a body, or matter, including an atom, molecule, neutron or proton, will not advance, progress, or move in a developing direction unless acted upon by an outside force, that it would be even more difficult for something that does not exist at all to take on existence, either suddenly or gradually, unless and until acted upon by some outside force. That problem leads inevitably to a discussion of "First Cause." What caused the first thing, whatever it was?

For this question, science has no genuine answers. The scientific world is filled, however, with multiplied unproved *hypotheses* which change with every decade and generation, all of which amount to nothing more than speculation and hyper-ventilated imagination wrapped in the protective aura and mystique of "science." The Bible speaks simply to this conundrum: "The fool hath said in his heart, There is no God" (Ps. 14:1, 53:1). In other words, only a fool could come to the conclusion that there is no Creator God because of the manifold evidence to the contrary, obvious to any truly honest man. As the apostle Paul noted, the very existence and operation of the material world that can be observed and experienced is sufficient to conclude any man or woman without excuse as to the existence and eternal power of God (Rom. 1:20). James goes further, stating that even the devils believe in God and tremble (Jam. 2:19).

Why, then, is the nineteenth century conception of Darwinism and the militant march of naturalism presented not as theory but as dogma? Why did the British *The Independent* announce, "World scientists unite to attack creationism?" Why did the national science academies of 67 countries warn parents and teachers to ensure that they did not undermine the teaching of evolution?[4] Why did they warn parents and teachers not to teach the concept of creation? What is driving this growing belligerence? Why are professors and researchers who even suggest the idea of "intelligent design" being fired and blacklisted worldwide?

Naturalism...is an alternative faith to Biblical Christianity, with its own "authoritative" teaching on the origins of all things material, shifting ultimate allegiance from a Creator God to Man as his own god.

The answer is quite simple. "It was apparent to many even in 1860—when the Anglican Bishop Samuel Wilberforce debated Darwin's defender Thomas Huxley at Oxford—that Darwin wasn't merely contradicting the literal Biblical account of a six-day creation...." As *NEWSWEEK* noted, he "appeared to undercut the very basics of Christianity, if not indeed all theistic religion." Was this "undercut" the natural consequence of a legitimate scientific fact or the promulgation of a theory intentionally designed to avert the implications of an omnipotent Creator for modern man? If there is no intent to foreclose honest inquiry, why then did The Quebec Ministry of Education tell Christian Evangelical schools that they "must teach Darwin's theory of evolution and sex education or close their doors…?"[5]

The true answer is that Naturalism is a non-theistic religion and belief system requiring immense faith, and is led by a passionate priesthood teaching and preaching the dogmas of Darwinism and humanism. It is an alternative faith to Biblical Christianity, with its own "authoritative" teaching on the origins of all things material, shifting ultimate allegiance from a Creator God to Man as his own god.

Eminent scientific philosopher and ardent Darwinist, Michael Ruse, even acknowledged that evolution is their religion!

> *Evolution is promoted by its practitioners as more than mere science. Evolution is promulgated as an ideology, a secular religion—a full fledged alternative to Christianity…. Evolution is a religion. This was true of evolution in the beginning and it is true of evolution still today.*[6]

Revealing the massive deception perpetuated upon an often unsuspecting, yet willing public, Richard Levontin of Harvard, left no doubt.

> *We take the side of science in spite of the patent absurdity of some of its constructs…in spite of the tolerance of the scientific community for unsubstantiated commitment to materialism…. We are forced by our a priori adherence to material causes to create an apparatus of investigation and set of concepts that produce material explanations, no matter how counterintuitive, no matter how mystifying to the uninitiated. Moreover, that materialism is absolute, for we cannot allow a Divine foot in the door.*[7]

This pseudo-scientific deception has seduced most of the academic world as well as the common man who bows at its shrine. Speaking of the trust students naturally place in their highly educated college professors, physicist Mark Singham blatantly admitted the intentional abuse of that trust by professors.

And I use that trust to effectively brainwash them... our teaching methods are primarily those of propaganda. We appeal—without demonstration—to evidence that supports our position. We only introduce arguments and evidence that supports the currently accepted theories and omit or gloss over any evidence to the contrary.[8]

Evolution is a religion...a religion without God. Julian Huxley, a primary architect of neo-Darwinism, called evolution a "religion without revelation" and wrote a book by that title. In that book, he argued passionately that we must change "our pattern of religious thought from a God-centered to an evolution-centered pattern."[9] Huxley then boldly declared the underlying motivation behind the dogma of evolution or naturalism that demands its tenets be preached. Please try to absorb the sheer arrogance of this deception.

"The God hypothesis...is becoming an intellectual and moral burden on thought." "We must construct something to take its place."[10]

The Heart of Deception

At the heart of deception lies a deceptive heart. The promulgators of evolution have chosen deception because they considered the alternative "religiously" intolerable. Robert Muller, a leader of the New Age movement and former assistant secretary general of the United Nations, said, "I believe the most fundamental thing we can do today is to believe in evolution…evolution is not merely a peripheral matter…, its basic in everything."[11]

Why is evolution considered "basic in everything" and "the most fundamental thing we can do?" The reason is quite simple. Evolution is not science but a philosophical and religious world view that precludes a Creator God who would have the authority to hold His creatures morally accountable to His own will. This is why Julian Huxley stated, "The God hypothesis is becoming an intellectual and moral burden." If the world is to create a global, godless system, defining its own "moral" standards rooted in sexual promiscuity and utopian unity that rejects the revealed truth of sin and salvation, the only alternative is naturalistic evolution to explain our existence.

In order for those intentionally self-deceived promoters of evolution to somehow live with themselves and promote their greater agendas, they need you to join them. If they can dupe the masses to democratically join them in the absurdity of their own deception, it somehow breathes legitimacy into a system that not only defies intellectual logic and mathematical probability but the most fundamental laws of science itself. Do we truly believe we can democratically overrule the laws of creation and the Creator by devising an artificial explanation for our existence, doubly deceiving ourselves by pretending it to be scientific? If you will believe this fundamental lie, what other lies are you prepared to believe built upon this lie?

FOUNDATION OF THE GLOBAL ORDER

Evolution does not stand alone. It is, as the former assistant secretary general of the United Nations noted, "the most fundamental thing we can do"…"to believe in evolution" as "basic in everything." To what is evolution so "basic"? It is basic to a new vision of man. It is basic to a vision of a global utopia, man-centered rather than God-centered. It is a satanic "salvation" being prepared for the world as an "acceptable" alternative to the hope of salvation in Jesus Christ.

The Humanist Manifesto II gives us a preview of the thinking undergirding this New World Order now exploding boldly into the Brave New World. Take thoughtful heed.

Traditional moral codes…fail to meet the pressing needs of today and tomorrow. False "theologies of hope" and messianic ideologies…cannot cope with existing world realities. They separate rather than unite peoples.

Humanity, to survive, requires bold and daring measures. We need to extend the uses of the scientific method…in order to build constructive social and moral values. Humanism can provide the purpose and inspiration that so many seek; it can give personal meaning and significance to human life.

We believe…that traditional dogmatic or authoritarian religions that place revelation, God, ritual, or creed above human needs and experience do a disservice to the human species. We can discover no divine purpose or providence for the human species…humans are responsible for what we are or will become. No deity will save us; we must save ourselves.[12]

Atheism in Disguise

Evolution is atheism in disguise. It is a religion in which man, having denied a Creator God, declares himself "god." Evolution is foundational to all fields of thought undergirding the rapidly advancing global evolutionary "church." The members of this "church" embrace man as the center of the universe and natural selection as their "creation story." Their priests are scientists and science teachers who have prostituted the legitimate purposes of science for an ulterior agenda. They preach their doctrine dogmatically, and will brook no opposition from within the ranks of science, labeling any who dare to suggest *Intelligent Design* or a Creator as a scientific "heretic," excommunicating them, burning their reputations at the stake.

> *Evolution is atheism in disguise...a religion in which man, having denied a Creator God, declares himself "god."*

Why the vengeance if this is science? It is because much more is at stake. Evolution is atheism in disguise, and those who promote it are at war with God. The atheistic nature of evolutionary thought is admitted, even insisted upon by most of its leaders. Ernst Mayr, for example, says that: "Darwinism rejects all supernatural phenomena and causations."[13] A professor in the Department of Biology at Kansas State University made clear:

> *Scientists and science teachers who have prostituted the legitimate purposes of science for an ulterior agenda...label any who dare to suggest Intelligent Design or a Creator as a scientific "heretic," excommunicating them, burning their reputations at the stake. Why the vengeance if this is science?*

Even if all the data points to an intelligent designer, such a hypothesis is excluded from science because it is not naturalistic.[14]

Evolution is, indeed, the false scientific basis of religious atheism. Will Provine at Cornell University frankly admits it. Consider the implications for your life, family and congregation.

As the creationists claim, belief in modern evolution makes atheists of people. One can have a religious view that is compatible with evolution only if the religious view is indistinguishable from atheism.[15]

A CHOICE FOR DESTINY

Evolution or naturalism is not simply a scientific viewpoint or theory that one can idly choose. The consequences of this choice are both temporal and eternal. To embrace evolution rather than Creation is to reject the fear of the Lord in order to embrace a false and fickle "science."

Evolution or naturalism is not simply a scientific viewpoint or theory that one can idly choose. The consequences of this choice are both temporal and eternal.

In the temporal realm of man's ongoing experience on this planet, evolutionary thinking has invaded and now pervades virtually every field of thought and endeavor, including the law. Nothing is deemed fixed or anchored in truth. Even the very concept of *truth* has largely vanished. *Truth* now is whatever I want it to be, morphing or *evolving* to suit the agenda *du jour*.

This abandonment of truth is leading inexorably to the embracing of a new evolving humanistic "truth," the revision of history, and the construction of a New Age utopian global order ostensibly to bring "salvation" to mankind and peace on earth through the New World Order announced over two hundred times by George Herbert Walker Bush during his presidency. At root is the religious belief of evolution. Julian Huxley, the first director general of UNESCO, could not have made it more plain.

We must develop a world religion of evolutionary humanism.[16]

The choice of evolutionary humanism as the world's religious belief system will culminate in a counterfeit (fake-real) christ promising peace on earth. That temporary peace, enforced by compelling every man, woman and child to submit, will explode in the greatest devastation and reign of terror ever experienced or conceived by man, for without God, every man does that which is right in his own eyes. He has become "god."

The choice of evolutionary humanism as the world's religious belief system will culminate in a counterfeit (fake-real) christ promising peace on earth.

The most devastating consequence remains. Eternity lies in the balance. One cannot embrace naturalistic evolution and the Word of God. They are mutually exclusive as clearly stated by evolution's strongest proponents. You must make a choice.

To choose evolution is to reject the God of Creation, the God of the Bible. The Bible declares that Jesus Christ created all things (Eph. 3:9, Col. 1:16). To embrace evolution is to reject Jesus Christ and to shift your worship to man. God's final warning to mankind before the outpouring of His wrath on the "children of disobedience" (those who refuse to humbly obey him) is a clear confrontation on the issue of creation. The Book of Revelation states that God will dispatch an angel to make one final plea to those on the earth, having "the everlasting gospel." Here is what the angel will say with a loud voice:

God's final warning to mankind before the outpouring of His wrath...is a clear confrontation on the issue of creation.

*Fear God, and give glory to him; for the hour of his judgment is come: and **worship him that made*** *heaven, and earth*, *and the sea, and the fountains of waters (Rev. 14:7).*

Whom you worship will determine your destiny. Those who believe in naturalistic evolution, by definition, cannot truly be worshipers of the God of Creation as revealed in the Scriptures. Will you worship man…or the Creator, God? Your viewpoint will determine your eternal destiny.

Postscript
Shocking…but true!

Darwin's theory—that humankind was the product of a slow, evolutionary process from early forms of life—conflicts with the literal biblical account of creation. Notwithstanding, on October 23, 1996, Pope John Paul II declared that now knowledge confirms the theory of evolution to be "more than a hypothesis." The Vatican is evolving, again, from the authority of Scripture to the authority of the Pope. On February 9, 2009, the Vatican under Pope Benedict XVI, "admitted that Charles Darwin was on the right track when he claimed that man descended from apes," also declaring Intelligent Design to be but a "cultural phenomenon" rather than either a scientific or theological issue. TIMESONLINE, timesonline. co.uk 2/11/09.

Has "science" supplanted the Creator? …Man's war against God is nearing the final battle. Where do you stand? Will you worship and serve the Creator, or the creature? The Secret of the Lord *awaits your decision.*

Has "science" supplanted the Creator? Apparently two popes now proclaim the *purity* of scientific theory trumps the proclamation of the Creator, thus elevating the viewpoint of the "Vicar of Christ" over Christ himself, who is declared by Scripture to be the creator of all things. Man's war against God is nearing the final battle. Where do you stand? Will you worship and serve the Creator, or the creature? *The Secret of the Lord* awaits your decision.

Chapter 20

PROVOCATIVE THOUGHTS FOR SECRET SEEKERS

1. In what ways has science become deceptive?

2. Why is the issue of the origin of man so critical to our eternal destiny?

3. What is the difference between a hypothesis or theory and truth? Why have so many become confused over the difference?

4. Do you find it surprising that virulent evolutionists would so blatantly admit that "evolution is a religion… a religion without God?"

5. Why would those promoting a new vision of man…a new global order…declare that the teaching and promotion of evolution is "the most fundamental thing we can do?"

6. Why are so many scientists so vengeful in seeking to keep God out of their considerations?

7. Can you see how the eternal and spiritual battle lines are being drawn? Which side are you on? In what way is your access to *The SECRET of the Lord* put at ultimate risk by your decision?

The Saving Secret

"By mercy and truth iniquity is purged: and by the fear of the Lord men depart from evil" (Prov. 16:6).

"The Secret of the Lord is with them that fear Him; and He will show them His covenant" (Psa. 25:14). "What man is he that feareth the Lord? Him shall He teach in the way that he shall choose. His soul shall dwell at ease; and his seed shall inherit the earth" (Psa. 25:12-13). "All the paths of the Lord are *mercy* and *truth* unto such as keep His covenant and His testimonies" (Psa. 25:10).

Mercy and Truth

If the heart of God toward you and me could be compressed and distilled into one simple expression, it would most likely be "mercy and truth." This pair of words echo continuously throughout Scripture, in both Old and New Testaments. The continuity is clear, because "Jesus Christ is the same yesterday, today and forever" (Heb. 13:8) in His oneness with God the Father.

This understanding of the indivisible and eternal wedding of *mercy* and *truth* in the character of God is essential for us to grasp the true nature of the "fear of the Lord" in the context of our faith-filled hope that *The Secret of the Lord* might be fully manifested in His holy, covenantal kindness toward those created in His image. God is character-bound by both *mercy* and *truth*. His mercy is manifested in His unbounded love, while His truth is manifested in justice, judgment and the necessity of obedient faith to reciprocate His love in the establishment and preservation of our relationship with Him as Creator. Without God's *truth*, we can never know or comprehend His *love* and *mercy*.

If the heart of God toward you and me could be compressed and distilled into one simple expression, it would most likely be "mercy and truth."

Fleshly man, ungoverned by the Spirit of Christ, always expects the fruit of relationship without the root of reconciliation obtained through repentance necessary to validate God's truth. We demand the love and mercy of God while casually…or rebelliously…rejecting or ignoring His truth and holiness. In effect, we re-define God in a manner acceptable to our flesh, while rejecting His truth which alone can make us free in relationship with Him.

Paul warned us not to expect the manifestation of The Secret of the Lord…*unless we are walking "in the Spirit," rather than "in the flesh."*

For this reason, the apostle Paul warned us not to expect the manifestation of *The Secret of the Lord,* either in this life or in the life to come, unless we are walking "in the Spirit," rather than "in the flesh" (Rom. 8:4-14).

Be not deceived; God is not mocked: for whatsoever a man soweth, that shall he also reap.

For he that soweth to his flesh shall of the flesh reap corruption; but he that soweth to the Spirit shall of the Spirit reap life everlasting.

Let us not be weary in well doing: for in due season we shall reap, if we faint not (Gal. 6:7-9).

Consider again the psalmist who seeks to express God's heart bent upon our reconciled relationship with Him, conjoined in mercy and truth as well as in Spirit and truth.

*I will praise thee with my whole heart.... I will worship...and praise thy name for thy **lovingkindness** [mercy] and thy **truth**: for thou hast magnified thy Word above all thy name (Psa. 138:2).*

He will bless them that fear the Lord, both small and great (Psa. 115:13).

*O praise the Lord...all ye people. For His **merciful kindness** is great toward us: and the truth of the Lord endureth forever (Psa. 117:1-2).*

*O give thanks unto the Lord; for He is good: because His **mercy** endureth forever (Psa. 118:1).*

Because of our continuous propensity to embrace mercy without truth, we must both see and surrender to what the Psalmist concludes regarding the interrelationship of mercy and truth. Again, we revel in mercy but are prone to revile truth. "O give thanks unto the Lord; for He is good," exhorts the psalmist, "because his mercy endureth forever." For God's mercy we must be forever grateful, for we are aware that without His mercy, we are without hope.

Yet the same psalmist follows with these seemingly strange words…

*Let them now that **fear** the Lord say, that his mercy endureth forever (Psa. 118:4).*

Why would he introduce the "fear" factor when reveling in the mercy of the Lord? It is because it is only in the stark reality of God's truth that mercy is mandated and has "moment" in our lives. It is *the fear of the Lord* that enables us to keep God's truth in proper balance and focus. We cannot whimsically cast ourselves upon God's mercy without the gripping, directing, cleansing and convicting power of His truth that causes us to truthfully cry for and claim His proffered mercy.

Mercy Without Fear

God's "mercy is on them that fear Him" (Luke 1:50). And our "fear" of the Lord is made manifest in and through our obedience to His truth. Without the heart-connecting link of God's truth which demands obedience, mercy becomes nothing but emotional sentimentality. And emotional sentimentality has no saving force in our lives. It is self-generating. It merely salves our feelings. Such mind-constructed "mercy" becomes deceptive self-manipulation, masking the true need for mercy. And we need mercy more than most are willing to admit.

The genuine fear of the Lord will drive us in abject humility, confessing our sin in deep repentance, to embrace God's mercy.

We must come clean before God. "For thou, Lord, art good, and ready to forgive; plenteous in mercy unto all them that call upon thee" (Psa. 86:5). The genuine fear of the Lord will drive us in abject humility, confessing our sin in deep repentance, to embrace God's mercy. Never in human history has there been greater need to "unite [our] hearts to fear thy name" that we might rightly claim His mercy (Psa. 86:11).

FEAR WITHOUT MERCY

Fear without mercy is eternal hopelessness, depriving us of the relationship of reconciliation so craved by our Creator. Fear without mercy is unremitting terror. It leads not to the triumph of God's love but to unrelenting tyranny of the soul in condemnation. Therefore, God, in divine compassion, tempers the ultimate mandate of His truth with love revealed in mercy. He does not demand the death penalty that our sin requires (Rom. 6:23), but rather extends forgiveness through His mercy…IF…we will come clean and confess (without excuse) our sin. Receiving the Messiah's sacrifice on the cross as the substitution for our well-deserved judgment, we (by simple faith) receive His merciful salvation, recognizing that, in merging His character of both mercy and truth, "He is faithful and just to forgive our sins, and to cleanse us from all unrighteousness" (I Jn. 1:9).

The fear of the Lord then becomes the initiating factor to place us in conscious recognition of our need for mercy. The mercy and grace of God then opens the door to access *The Secret of the Lord.* If we forsake the fear of the Lord, we frustrate His grace and foolishly demean His mercy.

> *The fear of the Lord… becomes the initiating factor to place us in conscious recognition of our need for mercy. If we forsake the fear of the Lord, we frustrate His grace and foolishly demean His mercy.*

THE SAVING SECRET

The *fear of the Lord* has a divinely-intended focus. The ultimate focus is to drive us to genuine faith revealed in loving

Mankind has always been confronted with the clear choice between the fear of God and the fear of man. That choice is now coming rapidly to its historic and prophetic culminating moment.

obedience to Jesus Christ, the Messiah, that will save us not only from hell fire but from being engulfed by the tyrannizing and paralyzing fear of man which will ultimately consign us to eternal perdition. Mankind has always been confronted with the clear choice between the fear of God and the fear of man. That choice is now coming rapidly to its historic and prophetic culminating moment. It is the ultimate moment of truth, and will be made in the valley of decision...your decision, and mine.

Do you fear God...or man? The fear of man is an eternal snare because it is choreographed by the Deceiver who has determined to destroy you while falsely promising to save through his coming earthly global government purporting to guarantee "security and prosperity" (Prov. 29:25). The fear of the Lord, on the other hand, leads to life and eternal salvation.

The choice is ours. The fear of man leads first to frustration, culminating in final damnation. The fear of God clears our minds and hearts to conform our thinking and ways to those of our Creator, culminating in conviction of sin, restoration of relationship with God, and eternal salvation. The choice cannot be avoided. Finding *The Secret of the Lord* through the fear of the Lord will be demonstrated first in a clean conscience and revived heart, uniting your spirit with God's Spirit in joyful reconciliation and peace, paving the way to the eternal presence of God.

Why, then, under heaven, would any man or woman choose rather to fear man? There are two simple reasons. First, those who ultimately fear man do not truly fear God as GOD. Second, those who resolve decisions in favor of the fear of man do not truly live by faith but rather by feelings. Upon close and honest analysis, piercing to the heart, where do *you* find yourself? Do not answer too quickly! You may wish to present this matter to the Lord in the privacy of your innermost being.

THE REVIVING SECRET

Many have cried out for moral and spiritual revival in America over this past generation. Some have almost bragged about the sheer volume of prayer arising from the lips of professing Christians in a plaintiff cry for revival and renewal. Yet, if we are truly honest, we have seen neither the root nor the fruit in measurable and observable reality of such revival. Why might that be? It is because,

We purport to worship God in spirit, but have, in practical ways, virtually relegated the God of truth to the archives of history.

in primary measure, we have either lost or outright abandoned the fear of the Lord from pastor to people. We purport to worship God in spirit, but have, in practical ways, virtually relegated the God of truth to the archives of history.

Once again the psalmist comes to the rescue. Be encouraged as you read and meditate upon his merciful words of hope and healing. First comes our groaning pleas, "Turn us, O God of our salvation; and cause thine anger toward us to cease. Wilt thou not revive us again; that thy people may rejoice in thee? Shew us thy mercy, O Lord, and grant us thy salvation" (Psa. 85:4-7).

We then must prepare, with the psalmist, to set our hearts for God's response. Can you join him? "I will hear what God the Lord will speak: for He will speak peace unto His people, and to His saints: but let them not turn again to folly" (Psa. 85:8). Notice, then, the fulcrum, of reviving faith. It is the fear of the Lord.

*Surely **His salvation is nigh them that fear Him**; that glory may dwell in our land (Psa. 85:9).*

> *If America, or any nation, hopes to see God's blessing and glory in the land, the fear of the Lord must first be restored. Revival will come on its heels.*

That's it! *The Secret of the Lord* and His salvation, whether temporal or eternal, is directly linked to the genuine fear of the Lord. If America, or any nation, hopes to see God's blessing and glory in the land, the fear of the Lord must first be restored. Revival will come on its heels.

Consider the gracious words of the psalmist as he resolves that the fear of the Lord must regain prominence for God's promises to be released.

*Mercy and **truth** are met together; righteousness and peace have kissed each other.*

Truth shall spring out of the earth; and righteousness shall look down from heaven.

Yea, the Lord shall give that which is good; and our land shall yield her increase.

Righteousness shall go before Him; and shall set us in the way of His steps (Psa. 85:10-13).

THE SECRET CONCLUSION

The words "fear of the Lord" or similar words describing the need for us to "fear God" occur not less than 179 times throughout the Bible. It is a continuous direction-setting, life and destiny-determining theme. It is the axis, from God's viewpoint, around which His wheel of salvation turns.

God is both a God of love and judgment. He is a God self-defined as fully mercy and fully truth. He is a God of deliverance to His saints who truly fear Him, yet He is a God of wrath for destruction to the wicked. The New Testament writer of Hebrews made abundantly clear that the God of Creation and of the Tanakh (Old Testament) is the same God found in the New Testament, "For our God is a consuming fire" (Heb. 12:29).

This New Testament writer then reminds us of our own time. He warns, "See that ye refuse not Him that speaketh. Whose voice then [at Mt. Sinai] shook the earth: but now He hath promised, saying, Yet once more I shake not the earth only, but also heaven. Wherefore…let us have grace, whereby we may serve God acceptably with reverence and godly fear" (Heb. 12:25-28).

We will either fear God acceptably, or fear man unacceptably. We now…must make a decision upon which rides our destiny.

We will either fear God acceptably, or fear man unacceptably. We now, at this moment of both history and prophecy, must make a *decision* upon which rides our *destiny*. It is directly related to the most fundamental *duty* of man.

Let us hear the conclusion of the whole matter: Fear God and keep His commandments: for this is the whole duty of man (Eccl. 12:12).

Chapter 21

PROVOCATIVE THOUGHTS FOR SECRET SEEKERS

1. Why do we tend to accept God's *mercy* while rejecting His *truth*?

2. Does it seem strange that God would tell us that His "mercy is on them that fear Him?" Why…or why not?

3. Why is mercy, without the heart-connecting link to Gods truth and required obedience, nothing but "emotional sentimentality?"

4. What happens in our hearts and minds when we are driven solely by fear…even the fear of the Lord…without embracing His offer of mercy?

5. What is the "divinely-intended focus" of the fear of the Lord?

6. How is the hope of a national restoration and revival dependant upon the recovery of the fear of the Lord… first among professing Christians?

7. What is "the whole duty of man?"

"LET US HEAR the conclusion of the whole matter: Fear God, and keep his commandments: for this is the whole duty of man.

For God shall bring every work into judgment, with every secret thing, whether it be good, or whether it be evil." Eccl. 12:13-14

Endnotes

Chapter 1

1. David A. Kaplan and Anna Underwood, "The Iceberg Cometh", *Newsweek*, Nov. 25, 1996, pp.68-73.
2. Stephen Cox, *Richmond Times Dispatch*, April 15, 2001, p. F3.
3. David A. Kaplan and Anna Underwood, *Newsweek*, p. 69.
4. Ibid, p. 73.
5. Ibid, p. 69.
6. Bob Garner, "Lessons From the Titanic," *Focus on the Family*, April 1997, p. 1-3.
7. Kim Masters, "Glub, Glub, Glub….", *TIME*, Nov. 25, 1996, p. 104.
8. Bob Garner, "Lessons From the Titanic," *Focus on the Family*, p. 2.
9. Ibid, p. 3.
10. Graham Tibbetts, "Key That Could Have Saved the Titanic," *Telegraph.co.uk*, August 30, 2007.
11. Brad Matsen, *Titanic's Last Secrets* (New York, Twelve, Hatchette Book Group, 2008), back cover.
12. Ibid.
13. Ibid, p. 227.
14. Ibid, p. 261.
15. Ibid, p. 238-39.
16. Ibid, p. 241.
17. Ibid, p. 239.
18. Ibid, p. 261.

Chapter 20

1. Jerry Adler, "Evolution of a Scientist," *NEWSWEEK*, November 28, 2005, Cover Story, pp. 51-58, p. 54.

2. Ibid, p. 55.
3. Henry Morris, *Steeling the Mind of America*, New Leaf Press, June 1995, p. 205-206.
4. Sarah Cassidy, "World Scientists Unite to Attack Creationism," *The Independent*, Online Edition, June 22, 2006, p. 1.
5. David Rogers, news story posted by *National Post* and Can West News Service online at www.canada.com, October 24, 2006, p. 6-7 as printed out.
6. Ernst Mayer, "Darwin's Influence on Modern Thought," *Scientific American* (vol. 283, July 2000), p. 83.
7. Richard Levontin, *Review of the Demon-Haunted World*, by Carl Sagan, In *New York Review of Books*, January 9, 1997.
8. Mark Singham, "Teaching and Propaganda," *Physics Today*, (vol. 53, June 2000), p. 54.
9. Julian Huxley, *Essays of a Humanist* (New York: Harper and Row, 1964), p. 222.
10. Ibid.
11. Henry Morris, *Steeling of the Mind of America*, New Leaf Press, June 1995, p. 220-221.
12. *Humanist Manifesto II*, 1973.
13. Ernst Mayer, "Darwin's Influence on Modern Thought," *Scientific American* (vol. 283, July 2000), p. 83.
14. Scott C. Todd, "A View from Kansas on the Evolution Debates," *Nature* (vol. 401, September 30, 1999), p. 423.
15. Will Provine, "No Free Will," in *Catching up with the Vision*, ed. By Margaret W. Rossiter (Chicago: University of Chicago Press, 1999), p. S123.
16. Henry Morris, *Steeling of the Mind of America*, New Leaf Press, June 1995, p. 215.

About the Author

For a veteran trial attorney to be referred to as "a prophet for our time" is indeed unusual, but many who have heard Charles Crismier's daily radio broadcast, *VIEWPOINT*, believe just that. Now, in *The SECRET of The LORD*, his words, full of "passion and conviction," provide clear direction to both seekers and professing believers increasingly drawn into the deceptive ways of the rapidly-developing new global order.

Crismier speaks from an unusual breadth of experience. After nine years as a public schoolteacher, he spent twenty years as a trial attorney, pleading causes before judge and jury. As a pastor's son, also serving in pastoral roles for 25 years, Crismier has been involved with ten distinct Protestant denominations—both mainline and otherwise, together with other independent and charismatic groups from coast to coast and from North to South—providing an enviable insider's view of American Christianity and life.

Deeply troubled by the direction of the nation and Church he loves, this attorney left his lucrative Southern California law practice in 1992 to form SAVE AMERICA Ministries and was awarded the Valley Forge Freedom

Foundation award for his contribution to the cause of "Rebuilding the Foundations of Faith and Freedom." "Chuck probes the heart and conscience of our nation and the Church with both a rare combination of insight, directness, urgency and compassion, and a message that desperately needs to be heard and heeded before it is too late."

From the birthplace of America—Richmond, Virginia—this former attorney speaks provocatively and prophetically on daily national radio as "a Voice to the Church," declaring "Vision for the Nation" in America's greatest crisis hour, preparing the way of the Lord for history's final hour.

Charles Crismier can be contacted by writing or calling:

P.O. Box 70879
Richmond, VA 23255
(804) 754-1822
crismier@saveus.org

or through his website at
www.saveus.org

Other Life-Changing Books
by Charles Crismier

SEDUCTION of the SAINTS
Staying Pure in a World of Deception

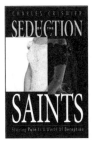

"Take heed that no man deceive you," declared Jesus just before his crucifixion. His words were chilling! They cast a frame around life and eternity. In the final moments of his life on earth, Jesus chose to leave the disciples, with whom he had invested his life and ministry, a penetrating and haunting warning they would never forget...a warning that echoes through the centuries to all his disciples preparing for the end of the age.

$ 18

RENEWING the SOUL of AMERICA
(Endorsed by 38 National Christian Leaders)

"As a country and as individuals, we stand at a crossroads—to continue on the path to godlessness or to return to the way of righteousness." "Renewing the Soul of America is America's ONLY hope." But it must begin with you...one person at a time. Powerful inspiration for these difficult times.

$ 18

OUT of EGYPT
Building End-time Trust for End-time Trials.

Liberating... yet sobering. If Abraham, Moses, Israel, and...yes, Jesus had to "come out Egypt," how about us? The words "out of Egypt" or similar words appear over 400 times from Genesis to Revelation. Why has this theme been mentioned perhaps more than any other in the entire Bible? You will read... and re-read this book!

$ 17

The POWER of HOSPITALITY
An Open Heart, Open Hand and Open Home Will Change Your World

 The Apostle Paul reminds that ALL who claim Christ as savior must, as a demonstration of their faith, be "given to hospitality." Pastors and leaders are to be "lovers of hospitality" as a condition of leadership. And Peter said, "The end of all things is at hand,... therefore use hospitality." Here is life-changing inspiration... PRACTICAL, PERSONAL and PROPHETIC.

$ 16

**Find them ALL at saveus.org
or call SAVE AMERICA Ministries 1 (800) SAVEUSA**